D0078473

The Manchester Ship Canal and the rise of the Port of Manchester 1894–1975

John K. Bythell, Chairman of the Manchester Ship Canal Company 1894–1916 and 'the second founder of the Manchester Ship Canal'. (*Manchester Ship Canal Company*).

The Manchester Ship Canal and the rise of the Port of Manchester 1894–1975

D. A. FARNIE

Manchester University Press

Copyright © D. A. Farnie 1980

Published by
Manchester University Press
Oxford Road, Manchester M13 9PL.

British Library cataloguing in publication data

Farnie, Douglas Antony.
The Manchester Ship Canal and the rise of the Port of Manchester, 1894–1975.
1. Manchester, Eng. – Docks – History.
2. Manchester Ship Canal – History.
I. Title.
387.1'09427'33 HE558.M/

ISBN 0–7190–0795–X

HE
558
.M35
F37
1980

Filmset by August Filmsetting, Reddish, Stockport.
Printed in Great Britain
by J. W. Arrowsmith Limited
Winterstoke Road, Ashton, Bristol

Contents

List of tables

List of illustrations

List of abbreviations

B.O.D.	Minutes of the Board of Directors of the Manchester Ship Canal Company
c.i.f.	cost, insurance, freight
f.o.b.	free on board
M.C.A.B.	Minutes of the Board of Directors of the Manchester Cotton Association
M.L.B.	Minutes of the Board of Directors of Manchester Liners
T.L.P.C.	Minutes of the Traffic, Land and Parliamentary Committee of the Manchester Ship Canal Company
T.R.C.	Minutes of the Traffic and Rates Committee of the Manchester Ship Canal Company

Preface

This short work seeks to make a contribution to history in the broadest sense rather than to the specialised field of transport history. It began as a study of the Manchester Ship Canal but evolved, with the growth of understanding in the author's mind, into a history of the Port of Manchester. Most accounts of the Ship Canal are based upon printed sources and indeed upon a single book. They narrate the story of the construction of the waterway but they tend to consider it almost as a 'thing-in-itself' and they lay no special emphasis upon the uniqueness of the achievement they relate. The comparative study of British ports by James Bird remains the sole exception to this generalisation. The present work does not attempt to summarise once more the two volumes compiled by Bosdin Leech. Indeed, it may be considered as a supplement to the work of Leech, which concludes with the election as chairman of the Ship Canal Company of John K. Bythell. Thus it begins with the opening of the Canal to traffic and the historic election of Bythell as chairman. Inevitably it excludes from its purview not only the history of construction but also the pre-history of the Canal (1712–1876) and the pre-history of the port (1844–60).[1] Essentially it seeks to examine what happened after the ceremonies of inauguration had ended. Such a tentative exploration into relatively unknown territory is inspired by no 'ignorant passion for originality'[2] but by a simple wish to relate the history of the port to the world which it served.

Shortage of space has entailed the virtual exclusion from consideration of

1 *Manchester Guardian*, 22 January 1861, 3vii; 10 September 1873, 6iv, and A. Redford and B. W. Clapp, *Manchester Merchants and Foreign Trade, Vol. II, 1850–1939* (Manchester University Press, 1956), 178, on the 'forgotten pioneer' William Gibb (1800–73), the wine and spirit merchant, who secured the Inland Bonding Act of 1860.

2 P. Rieff, *Fellow Teachers* (London, Faber, 1975), 16.

certain aspects of the subject, including the Bridgewater Canal, the canalside towns and the respective roles of capital and labour in the operation of the port. This book does not purport to be a business history of the Ship Canal Company and does not try to relate its complex financial history, in part from a belief that the benefits of the new port were diffused so widely as to leave for long but meagre monetary returns to the Company's ordinary shareholders. The intention has been to sketch the history of the port in terms of the staples of its traffic and of the main trends in its activity, especially in so far as they reflect the two great tidal currents of the modern world economy, the flow of cotton manufactures in the nineteenth century and the flow of oil in the twentieth.

Since this book is based primarily upon manuscript material rather than upon printed sources I must acknowledge with a profound sense of gratitude the permission generously granted by Mr D. K. Redford, the Chairman of the Ship Canal Company, to consult the minutes of the board of directors. I have also been very kindly granted access to the minutes of the board of directors of Manchester Liners Ltd by the former Chairman, Mr R. B. Stoker, and the Secretary, Mr D. Porter. I am indebted to Mr A. F. Mack, the Director of the Manchester Chamber of Commerce, for permission to consult the minutes of the Port of Manchester Committee, to Mr G. Pitt, the Secretary of the North West Timber Trade Association, for access to the minutes of the Manchester Timber Trade Association and to the Town Clerk of the City of Manchester, for enabling me to consult the proceedings of the Special Committees of Manchester Corporation. Miss Jean Ayton, the Archivist of the City of Manchester, and Mr Andrew Cross, the Archivist of the City of Salford, have very kindly made available additional manuscript material and have permitted its use in this publication. It has been a considerable privilege to undertake research in one of the world's great libraries, the Manchester Central Library, whose staff have maintained the great tradition established by Edward Edwards (1812–86) and have produced a wealth of material with speed, efficiency and courtesy. I must acknowledge in particular the help readily afforded upon countless occasions by Mr H. Horton of the Social Sciences Library. Two Local History Libraries have provided valuable assistance, that at Manchester with its abundant resources and that at Salford with its ever-helpful staff, especially Mr J. L. Shirt. To the Ship Canal Company I am indebted for permission to reproduce many illustrations of the Canal. Mr R. H. Offord of Manchester University Press suggested the original idea for this book and has been consistently helpful during the process of production, not least with the illustrations. Finally I must express my deepest thanks to Mr A. O'Brien, Assistant to the Secretary of the Ship Canal Company, Mr R. A. H. Collinge, for the aid he has so liberally and kindly extended upon my visits to Ship Canal House. Without the assistance of Mr O'Brien this work could never have been completed. I am grateful to Mr Redford, Mr Collinge and Mr O'Brien for reading the original draft of this work but I must add that the Ship Canal Company bears no responsibility for any personal opinion expressed in the following pages.

Any improvement which would enable vessels of 400 to 500 tons burthen to discharge their cargoes in a *commodious wet dock at Hulme*, would form an epoch of such magnitude in the history of Manchester, as would quadruple her population, and render her the first as well as the most enterprising city in Europe. [*The Annals of Electricity, Magnetism, and Chemistry* . . . conducted by William Sturgeon, Vol. VI, May 1841, 363, William Fairbairn, 'On the Improvement of the Mersey and Irwell Navigation', 8 February 1841]

Lancashire remains the nursery of transport evolution, which it has been for so many decades of history. [*Journal of the Institute of Transport*, January 1921, 112, E. S. Shrapnell-Smith, C.B.E., 'The Manchester Ship Canal as a Factor in Transport']

I

The Ship Canal Company and the Corporation of Manchester

During the nineteenth century Manchester had become an economic power-house and an object of hypnotic fascination to outside observers. In 1894 this unique city accomplished a feat without precedent in modern history by transforming itself through its own initiative and its own resources into an inland port, fifty-five miles from the open sea. The construction of the Manchester Ship Canal was the most distinctive feature of a marked revival of economic activity which ended an era of profound depression in local trade. The renaissance of the 1890s did not begin in the cotton industry but in its associated trades, in engineering, commerce and finance, in a large expansion of municipal activity and in a building boom which paved the way for a notable growth of population in 1901–11. The extension of the municipal boundary in 1889–90 ushered in a generation of rising ratable values after a decade of stagnation and created the idea of a 'Greater Manchester' of two million people, all within walking distance of the Royal Exchange.[1] The completion in 1894 of the Thirlmere aqueduct and of the Davyhulme sewage works immediately improved the material condition of the local population while the opening of the Ship Canal enhanced its prosperity in the longer term. Municipal enterprise was extended into new spheres, to aid the Ship Canal Company in 1891–93, to supply hydraulic power and electricity in 1894, to operate tramways in 1897, to establish Corporation housing at Blackley from 1902 and to buy in 1903 the near-by Heaton Park, which provided some compensation for the

[1] *Manchester City News*, 2 November 1889, 9i, 'Trafford Park for Greater Manchester'. *Manchester Guardian*, 13 September 1894, 8vi, J. W. Harvey.

loss of Trafford Park in 1896. So notable an extension of 'municipal socialism' (1885) created one of the strongest civic authorities ever known, necessitated the elaboration of a six-volume Manchester Municipal Code (1892–1901) and began to undermine the individualism of traditional 'Manchesterdom' (1882).

In an age of unprecedented technological progress the completion of the Ship Canal represented a great triumph for both civil and mechanical engineering and stimulated a general expansion of machine technology. 'It made Manchester the greatest engineering city in the world.'[2] Textile machine-making enjoyed a boom created by the expansion of the cotton industry abroad, technical colleges were established in both Manchester and Salford in 1895–96 and electrical engineering experienced rapid development from 1896. The establishment in 1896–97 of the world's first industrial estate in Trafford Park, hard by the Ship Canal, ushered in a new industrial era in the history of Manchester in succession to the commercial era of 1820–1900, shifting the city's economic centre of gravity from the north-east towards the rural south-west. In the sphere of commerce a notable expansion of the distributive trades was fostered by the completion of the Ship Canal. Local trade associations were formed by fruit merchants, cotton merchants and steamship owners in 1894, by timber merchants and bankers in 1895 and by provision dealers in 1899. In the financial field a great flotation boom in 1898 established the trust in the finishing industries, inspired efforts to create combinations in many other trades, including bill-posting,[3] and marked the beginning of a revolution in business organisation. Manchester became one of the great 'tentacular cities' of the modern age not only through its commercial and financial functions but also through its distributive trades, its Co-operative Wholesale Society, its trade associations and industrial trusts, its new electric tramways, its sale of

[2] W. H. Mills, *Sir Charles W. Macara, Bart.: a Study of Modern Lancashire* (Manchester, Sherratt, 1917), 138.

[3] A. L. Smyth, 'Youde's Billposting Journal', *Manchester Review*, 10, summer 1963, 47–50. *Northern Finance and Trade*, 17 November 1897, 405; 11 May 1898, 362, 364; 18 May, 383; 22 June, 465; 29 June, 481; 7 September, 645; 14 September, 664–5. *Manchester Guardian*, 3 November 1899, 4iv.

water from Thirlmere to other boroughs and its expanding cultural institutions, culminating in the establishment of an independent university with its own press in 1904. Newspapers enlarged their market through the enterprise of Edward Hulton (1869–1925) as well as of the 'new journalists' of the *Manchester Guardian*. The city made communications more than ever the basis of its economic empire: it remained 'an active manufactory of agitation and thought'[4] and extended its influence increasingly within Lancashire rather than within the wider world, supplying an appropriate seat for the Manchester school of hyperdiffusionism in anthropology, led by Grafton Elliot Smith (1871–1937).

The revival of commerce renewed the self-confident spirit of the 1840s, which was manifest most clearly in the claim that Manchester would make a more suitable capital city than London. 'It occupies, in point of fact, the exact centre of modern industrial and commercial Britain . . . London is a southern suburb of Lancashire and Yorkshire.'[5] To that outburst of euphoria the inauguration of the Ship Canal made a large contribution by transforming an inland metropolis of industry into a seaport and crowning the labours of twelve years. Four fierce battles had been fought and won by the supporters of the Canal to secure in succession the enabling Act of 1885, the necessary private capital in 1887, the construction of the great waterway and the financial aid from the municipality required to ensure its completion. Between 1887 and 1894 54 million cubic yards had been excavated, or half as much as was removed in the building of the Suez Canal and one-fifth of the amount dug out in the construction of the Panama Canal. The completed Canal was 35.5 miles long and, by August 1894, 26 ft deep,[6] or four times as deep as the channel of the former navigation. It used the water of the rivers Irwell and Mersey in order to link Manchester to Eastham on the Mersey estuary and

4 W. H. Mills, 'Manchester of Today', in H. M. McKechnie (ed.), *Manchester in 1915* (Manchester University Press, 1915), 9.

5 *Manchester Guardian*, 22 May 1894, 7ii, quoting Grant Allan 'Provincial London'.

6 Manchester Ship Canal Company, *Traffic and Rates Committee, Minutes* (hereafter cited as 'T.R.C.'), 152, 5 April 1894; 244, 7 June 1894; 54, 2 August 1894.

Directors' Meeting

At a Meeting of the Directors held at the Eastham Hotel, Eastham, on Friday, the 11th November 1887 at 1 o'clock.

Present:

Lord Egerton of Tatton in the Chair
Sir J. C. Lee
Mr. W. H. Bailey
,, H. Boddington
,, J. K. Bythell
,, W. J. Crossley
,, C. J. Galloway
,, J. Leigh
,, S. R. Platt
also ,, Saxon

Previous to the meeting the Board took the opportunity of inspecting a portion of the land recently acquired by the Company and the plant which had been brought on the ground by the Contractor.

There were present on the ground besides the Directors Mr. J. E. Platt (recently retired from the Board) Mr. E. Leader Williams, Chief Engineer, Mr. J. Abernethy, Consulting Engineer, Mr. W. J. Saxon, Solicitor, Mr. A. M. Dunlop, Land Agent, Mr. Marshall Stevens, Messrs. George Hicks and Bosdin T. Leech, Auditors, Mr. W. H. Hunter, Chief Assistant Engineer and Mr. A. H. Whitworth, Secretary.

Mr. T. A. Walker the Contractor together with his representative Mr. Topham and other Assistants was also present - an ordinary Navvy's spade having been provided the Chairman, Lord Egerton, cut the first sod of the undertaking in the centre of the site of the entrance locks. The Deputy Chairman cut the second sod and was followed by each of the other Directors present who filled an ordinary navvy's barrow which was wheeled and tipped by Mr. E. Leader Williams.

The beginning of construction works, 1887 (*Manchester Ship Canal Company, Minutes of the Board of Directors, 11 November 1887, 228*). Sir Joseph C. Lee, the chairman of Tootal's served from 1887 to 1893 as the deputy chairman of the board of twelve directors. The directors included the Mayor of Stockport, Joseph Leigh, and the Mayor of Oldham, S. R. Platt. The three absent directors were all elderly persons: Jacob Bright, M.P., Charles Moseley and John Rylands. James Abernethy (1814–96), the consulting engineer, had decided in 1882 in favour of E. L. William's idea of a locked canal and against H. Fulton's impracticable idea of a tidal cut. Other accounts of the ceremony are in the *Manchester Guardian*, 12 November 1887, 5v, and in B. T. Leech, *History of the Manchester Ship Canal* (Manchester, Sherratt, 1907), ii, 17–18.

---

divided the rise of 60.5 ft from sea level among four sets of locks. The State set its official seal of approval upon the joint work of the Canal Company and the Corporation. On 22 December 1893 the city's first lord mayor received a Treasury warrant dated 18 December which constituted Manchester a customs port with effect from 1 January 1894, and so created a new lawful place of entry to, and exit from, the realm for persons and merchandise.[7] The new port extended along the whole length of the Canal from Pomona to Eastham and formed 'for all practical purposes a Dock from end to end, 35 miles in length'.[8] It also included the estuary of the Mersey as far as an imaginary line drawn from Dungeon Point to Ince Ferry, which marked the respective limits of the two ports of Liverpool and Manchester. The eastern limits of the port of Liverpool were moved eleven miles westwards from Warrington. The port of Manchester absorbed the port of Runcorn, created in 1862,[9] and included the rivers Mersey, Irwell and Weaver as far as Frodsham. The legal limits of a port had been established: the new task of the Canal Company was to make a legal creation into an economic reality and to justify the appointment of an independent collector of customs revenue.[10]

The primary function of the Canal was to reduce the costs of transport and to do so permanently. Any estimate of the social

[7] Manchester Ship Canal Company, *Board of Directors, Minutes* (hereafter cited as 'B.O.D.'), 420–1, 10 November 1893; 453, 22 December 1893; 31, 16 February 1894; 46, 2 March 1894.

[8] Manchester Ship Canal Company, *Preliminary Prospectus*, 8 October 1885.

[9] B.O.D., 4–6, 19 January 1894.

[10] *Manchester City News*, 19 January 1895, 5v.

savings effected by the cutting of the Canal was, however, recognised by the best informed contemporary observer as a most difficult task.[11] The savings accomplished are to be measured not so much by the traffic handled by the Canal or by the dividends distributed by the Canal Company as by the competitive lowering in the rates of carriage of all goods whether passing along the Canal or using alternative routes. Those reductions were effected in two phases, in 1883 and 1885 and in 1895 and 1896. The saving of 1*s* 6*d* per ton or 31 per cent on four million tons of traffic between Manchester and Liverpool, of which the Ship Canal carried 1.5 million tons in 1896, achieved a minimum economy of £300,000 per annum:[12] other estimates raised the aggregate saving to £1,000,000 or even to £1,800,000.[13] The resulting reduction in the cost of carriage by all routes benefited both users and non-users of the Ship Canal at the expense of the railway companies[14] but halved the expected remuneration of the Canal Company.[15] Those concessions enabled Manchester shippers to cut their transit costs without changing their customary routes and to squeeze both ship owners and the Canal Company to the utmost. 'They seem to look upon the Ship Canal simply as a weapon for obtaining concessions from the old routes.'[16] The Canal Company dared not, however, contemplate, let alone embark upon, a suicidal rate war with the railways, the dock companies and the ship owners of England, representing an aggregate capital of £2,000 million.[17] It had achieved its primary and essential object by bringing about a general and permanent reduction in railway and port charges. It could not, however, afford to compete for traffic on the Liverpool–Manchester route with the railways, upon

[11] *Manchester Guardian*, 2 April 1896, 7ii–iii, Alderman J. W. Southern, quoting W. H. Collier (1853–1919), manager of the Bridgewater Canal (1887–96) and of the Ship Canal (1897–1900).

[12] *Manchester Guardian*, 2 April 1896, 7ii–iii.

[13] *Northern Finance and Trade*, 31 July 1897, 40.

[14] *The Statist*, 8 December 1894, 687, 'The Manchester Ship Canal'.

[15] Manchester Ship Canal Company, *Report of the Directors*, 21 February 1900, 10; 8 August 1902, 7; 17 February 1903, 2, J. K. Bythell.

[16] Ibid., 28 February 1894, 4; 28 August 1894, 4; 24 August 1897, 10, J. K. Bythell. B.O.D., 281, 22 March 1895; 398, 16 August 1895; 8, 20 December 1895.

[17] T.R.C., 14–15, 12 January 1894; B.O.D., 176, 19 October 1894.

which it remained wholly dependent for the expansion of the hinterland of the port of Manchester. Not only would a rate-cutting war have been impossible to win but it would also have reduced tolls to an unremunerative level, sacrificed revenue essential for the expansion of the Company's services and precluded the Company from ever again raising tolls. The Canal thus remained a potential route for commerce, a bridle upon both railway rates and shipping freights and a guarantee against any return to the monopolistic position of 1872–82.

The Canal served a symbolic as well as an economic function, exerting a powerful and sustained influence upon the imagination as a product of pure faith. As 'the People's Canal' it represented not only a triumph for the small shareholder[18] but also a bold experiment in municipal enterprise, providing in 'Manchester's mightiest undertaking'[19] a unique object of civic pride in a city where such symbols were few. 'The Canal is a labour of giants in engineering, in finance, and above all in civic energy and enterprise.'[20] 'So far as its navigableness is concerned, it will remain as the grandest undertaking ever realised in this country, and a permanent memorial of what may justly be described as the greatest non-martial triumph that has ever been witnessed.'[21] Manchester established a new pre-eminence, in municipal enterprise, and so stirred other towns to emulation. At the close of the boom of 1880–83 in the projection of maritime canals Preston embarked on a ten-year plan to improve the navigation of the Ribble. Birmingham was encouraged by the beginning of the construction works to project its own ship canal to Manchester in 1887 and another to Weston on the Mersey in 1890.[22] Ship canals were also projected in Sheffield in 1888 and in Blackburn in 1891.[23]

18 *Manchester Courier*, 2 January 1894, 4vii.

19 *Manchester Guardian*, 26 October 1894, 7ii, Alderman Alexander Forrest, (1838–98), first president of the Ship Canal Shareholders' Association.

20 *Daily News*, 22 May 1894, 5i.

21 *Manchester City News*, 16 June 1894, 8vi, William Pinkney.

22 B.O.D., 247, 2 December 1887.

23 Ibid., 442, 17 August 1888. *The Bee. The Magazine of the Blackburn Technical School*, March 1891, 26–7, 'The Blackburn Ship Canal. An argument in three chapters'.

Other schemes sought to link Stockport by waterway and Oldham via a Chadderton–Royton–Castleton canal to the Ship Canal.[24] The successful inauguration of the Manchester Ship Canal, coupled with that of the Corinth Canal in 1893 and the Kiel Canal in 1895, encouraged the projection of ship canals in Europe by Marseilles, Rotterdam, Ghent, Bruges and Brussels: in America it evoked proposals for a Darien Canal, a Michigan–Detroit Canal and a New York–Philadelphia Canal. In Britain it stimulated suggestions for the construction of six other ship canals, from Wakefield and Sheffield to Goole, from Birmingham to Worcester, from the Bristol to the English Channel, from the Forth to the Clyde and from Dublin to Galway Bay.[25] Other schemes envisaged the 'dockization' of the Avon from Bristol to Avonmouth and the canalisation of the Dee from Chester to Mostyn.[26]

The Manchester Ship Canal Company acquired no peers and remained a unique institution, created by statute and financed by the capital of 39,000 shareholders, the largest number of investors in any private company. In the business world of Manchester the Company had no equal, since it did not originate as a family firm, it was dedicated to a service function and it was larger than any other firm, being allotted as the successor of the Bridgewater Trust special representation upon the board of the Chamber of Commerce. The functions performed by the Company became far more varied that it had ever envisaged, even within the rigid limits imposed by statute, and necessitated repeated resort to Parliament for supplementary enabling Acts. As the port and harbour authority, it was responsible for the operation of the whole port, for the regulation of navigation and for the implementation of successive works programmes. As a canal proprietor, it operated the locks and swing bridges, supplied pilots and tugs to ships and dredged the approach channel as well as the bed. It also issued rate schedules, received tolls on cargo, levied them on ships from 1901 and opened traffic accounts, so becoming a banker: it even undertook marine insurance between 1897 and 1909

[24] B.O.D., 231, 4 October 1889; 264, 15 February 1895; 276–7, 8 March 1895.
[25] *Manchester City News*, 17 March 1894, 5iv; 17 November 1894, 6iii.
[26] *Northern Finance and Trade*, 6 October 1897, 275, 296.

after a voyage on the Canal had been assimilated to one upon the high seas.[27] In 1887 it had acquired the Bridgewater Canal, which supplied 'an essential valuable adjunct'.[28] and generated more gross revenue than the Ship Canal itself until 1901 but suffered a decline in its net receipts by 58 per cent between 1894 and 1901. As a dock company it co-ordinated all the services available within the terminal docks in order to ensure a speedy turn-round of vessels. Until 1947 it remained the sole employer of all dock labour, free from competition by either stevedores or master porters, unlike in London or Liverpool.[29] It recognised the dockers' union in 1911 and accepted the principle of the closed shop in 1919 but early developed the mechanical handling of coal, grain and oil. The Canal Company also secured recognition in 1897 by the railway companies as a railway company, followed by the grant of Clearing House privileges in 1907, and built up the largest private railway system in the world. In the handling of cargo the company acted as a warehousing, forwarding and shipping agent as well as bailee. It recruited railway rates clerks on a large scale in order to handle the letters which were pouring into the docks office by 1914 at the daily rate of 1,600.[30] As a landlord, the Company owned 4,664 acres acquired for the construction of the Canal at an average cost of £291 per acre, received chief rents and granted rights of way across its property. That particular function was extended by the purchase in 1921 of the Barton Dock Estate of 1,000 acres and by the erection of Ship Canal House (1924–26) in the financial heart of Manchester.

During the final phase of construction between 1891 and 1893 the Canal Company had become a dyarchy unique in British history. The Corporation of the City of Manchester, on the advice of its own Ship Canal Committee established in 1891,[31] advanced to the Com-

[27] B.O.D., 142–3, 24 August 1894; 333–4, 24 December 1909.

[28] Manchester Ship Canal Company, 'Report and Appendices on Bridgewater Revenue and Traffic', 11 January 1902, 14, J. K. Bythell.

[29] Manchester Ship Canal Company, *Traffic Land and Parliamentary Committee* (hereafter cited as 'T.L.P.C.'), 69–73, 11 August 1893; 139–40, 6 October 1893.

[30] Manchester Ship Canal Company, *Report of the Directors*, 25–26 February 1915, 8, J. K. Bythell on the 1,600 letters and the 3,000 accompanying documents.

[31] Manchester Corporation, *Proceedings of Special Committees*, vol. 2 (1890–93), 27–8, 3 February 1891.

Latchford cutting, 1893 (*Leech, op. cit., ii, 32*). 'On the 20th November [1893] the actual filling of the last section [from Runcorn to Latchford] commenced, and one saw the bottom of the Ship Canal for the last time; there was really a melancholy interest in parting with an old friend. Those who in after years view the thirty-five miles of placid water will have little idea of the vast chasm beneath, every mile of it crowded with incidents of one kind or another . . . Few will ever realise the miles of contractor's railway lines or the army of navvies that once found occupation in the bottom of the canal'. (Leech, op. cit., ii, 164–5; *Manchester Guardian*, 21 November 1893, 4i.) The filling of the 55 ft deep Latchford cutting was completed by 2 December and made possible the voyage of the *Snowdrop* on 8 December.

pany £3 million in 1891–92 and a further £2 million in 1893–94, so supplying the Company with 32.5 per cent of its capital and enabling the work of construction to be completed under the masterful direction of Alderman Sir John Harwood (1832–1906).[32] The Corporation pledged its credit upon a heroic scale in order to preserve the prestige of the city and was even able to make a profit on the transaction by borrowing at 3 per cent the funds which it loaned out at

[32] *Manchester Guardian*, 16 April 1906, 10ii–iii.

$4\frac{1}{2}$ per cent. That loan gave the Company a distinctive capital structure wherein ordinary shares supplied only 26 per cent of the total capital of £15.4 million, preference shares provided another 26 per cent and mortgage debentures furnished the remainder. A Ship Canal Shareholders' Association was formed in 1892 in order to protect the interests of the ordinary shareholders:[33] it could not, however, prevent an increase in the number of Corporation directors from one-third of the board in 1891 to a majority of eleven out of twenty-one in 1893 in a fundamental and irreversible shift of control. Negotiations in London between the Company and the representatives of the preference shareholders lasted for ten days and ended in the agreement of 13 March 1893, by which the chairman of the Company would always be elected by the shareholders' directors and the deputy-chairman, until the repayment of the loan, by the Corporation directors.[34]

The Corporation increased the municipal rates by 26 per cent between 1892 and 1895 and doubled its municipal debt between 1891 and 1896 but moderated the impact of the increase by a large extension of the municipal boundary, so increasing the productive power of a penny rate and discouraging migration by the wealthy outside the limits of a high-rated town. It extended further aid to the Company by providing essential port facilities in 1894–97 and, above all, by allowing the $4\frac{1}{2}$ per cent interest due upon its debentures to fall into arrears. Those arrears of interest increased elevenfold from £168,750 at 31 December 1895 to £1,805,990 at 31 December 1904, while the Corporation imposed a special Ship Canal rate and paid £1,015,209 net from the rates during the eight and three-quarter years from 1 April 1896 to 31 December 1904 in order to make up the necessary interest at 3 per cent.[35]

A reorganisation of the financial relations between Company and Corporation became necessary as the burden of the Ship Canal rate grew while the Company remained committed to pay a high rent of 4.84 per cent to the Manchester Ship Canal Warehousing Company

33 Ibid., 15 December 1891, 5vii–viii; 13 February 1892, 9iv–vi.
34 B.O.D., 231, 17 March 1893.
35 Ibid., 76, 10 February 1905.

First Journey of Directors from Eastham to Manchester by water

The first journey of the Directors from Eastham to Manchester by water took place on the 7th inst. The journey was made in the s.s. "Snowdrop" belonging to the Wallasey Local Board. The following Directors and Officers of the Company were on board, some of whom had proceeded to Liverpool the previous night.

W. H. Bailey, Esq. (Mayor of Salford and Chairman of Finance Committee)
J. K. Bythell, Esq. (Chairman of the Traffic and Rates Committee)
W. J. Crossley, Esq.
C. J. Galloway, Esq. (Chairman of the Bridgewater Committee)
Alexander Henderson, Esq. *Sir E. G. Jenkinson, K.C.B.*
Sir Joseph C. Lee *Joseph Leigh, Esq. M.P.*
S. R. Platt, Esq.
The Right Honorable the Lord Mayor of Manchester
Alderman Sir John Harwood (Deputy Chairman of the Company)
Alderman Leech (Chairman of the Land and Estate Committee)
Alderman Mark *Alderman Clay*
Alderman Walton Smith
Councillor Southern (Chairman of Stores Committee)
Councillor McDougall *Councillor Pingstone also the Chief Engineer, Corporation Engineer, Manager, Solicitor, Land Agent, Mr. Schenk, Mr. Collier (Manager of the Bridgewater Undertaking) Mr. Topham and the Secretary.*

The "Snowdrop" left Prince's Landing Stage, Liverpool, at 7.30 a.m. and reached Eastham Locks at 8.4, Ellesmere Port at 8.30, Saltport at 9.14, Runcorn (Bridgewater House) at 9.37 (where the works in progress were inspected) Moore Lane Swing Bridge 10.28 (this Bridge was opened under one minute) Stag Inn Swing Bridge 10.41, Northwich Road Swing Bridge at 11.2, Knutsford Road Swing Bridge 11.18, Latchford Locks 11.22, Irlam Locks 12.30, Barton Locks 1 o'clock and Barton Swing Bridge and Barton Aqueduct at 1.24.

Immediately after passing the Aqueduct three cheers were heartily given for the Chief Engineer. Mode Wheel Locks were entered at 1.53 and the sluices, gates, Dry Dock and proposed site for the depôt for Foreign Cattle were inspected.

At 2.50 Dock No. 3 was reached and at 3.12 Dock No. 4.

There was no hitch or delay of any kind throughout the entire journey; the Swing Bridges were worked with ease and rapidity.

The first voyage along the Canal, 8 December 1893 (*Manchester Ship Canal Company, Minutes of the Board of Directors, 8 December 1893, 445*). Eighteen of the twenty-one directors partook in the voyage of the *Snowdrop*. The three absentees were two Corporation directors, Alderman Joseph Thompson and Alderman Stephen Chesters Thompson, leader of the Conservatives on the City Council, and the chairman of the board: Lord Egerton was questioning the Foreign Secretary in the House of Lords on the attitude of the Foreign Office towards the imminent opening of the Canal. Alderman Anthony A. Marshall (1826–1916) had become on 3 August 1893 the first Lord Mayor of Manchester. The five officials listed in the minute were E. Leader Williams (1828–1910), G. H. Hill (1828–1919), Marshall Stevens (1852–1936), W. J. Saxon (1851–94) and A. M. Dunlop. A. O. Schenk, one of the engineers of the contractor T. A. Walker (1828–89), had taken charge in 1892 of the reorganised dredging department. William Hampson Topham, a civil engineer and railway contractor, was chief agent for T. A. Walker (1887–89), works manager (1890–91) of the Canal Company and the successor of Abernethy as consulting engineer from 1892. Other accounts of the voyage may be found in the *Manchester Guardian*, 8 December 1893, 5iii; the *Manchester City News*, 9 December 1893, 8v, and Leech, op. cit., ii, 166–8. The voyage of the *Snowdrop* was followed by a visit of press representatives on 16 December, by the official constitution of the Port of Manchester by the Board of Customs on 21 December and by the opening of the Canal to traffic on 1 January 1894.

and proposed to extend the same 'leasing' principle to the construction of the new dock, No. 9.[36] In the ensuing debate rival proposals were made to increase the respective influence of private enterprise and of the municipality. Marshall Stevens proposed the separation of the Canal and the docks, the transfer of the docks to the Corporation and the construction of a public dock estate in Trafford Park.[37] Barrow I. Belisha (1854–1906) urged the purchase by the Corporation of the whole Canal undertaking and its administration as a municipal enterprise.[38] On behalf of the preference shareholders Sir Alexander Henderson (1850–1934) proposed a complete financial reorganisation by which the £5 million of Corporation debentures would be transferred in forty-three years' time to the ordinary and preference shareholders in return for an immediate payment of £750,000, which would pay for the new dock and would be the exact equivalent of a 4½ per cent debenture for £5 million deferred for forty-three years. That arrangement would virtually have handed over control of the Canal Company to the London financiers and would never have been accepted either by the Corporation or by the Manchester shareholders.[39] A special sub-committee of the Corporation was appointed on 25 June 1903 and favoured a scheme prepared by Alderman J. W. Southern (1840–1909)[40] but modified it in the interests of the shareholders by rejecting a proposal to reduce the face value of the ordinary shares and to waive the preferential quality of the existing preference shares. It accepted the proposal of J. K. Bythell, the chairman of the Company, that the Corporation debentures should be transformed into perpetual debentures but rejected his suggestions that the Corporation should accept ordinary

[36] Ibid., 7–14, 31 January 1902; 32–40, 18 February 1902. Manchester Corporation, *Report of the Ship Canal Committee*, 21 February 1902, 5–14.

[37] Manchester Ship Canal Company, *Report of the Directors*, 21 February 1900, 13; 8 August 1901, 11–13. B.O.D., 375, 31 December 1903; 379–80, 5 January 1904; 418–19, 25 March 1904.

[38] Manchester Ship Canal Company, *Report of the Directors*, 18 February 1904, 5–6.

[39] B.O.D., 262–3, 22 May 1903. *Manchester Guardian*, 17 June 1903, 10vi. *Manchester City News*, 15 August 1903, 4vi.

[40] *Manchester Guardian*, 11 January 1909, 4i–ii.

shares in lieu of arrears of interest and that all shares should be made into a single common stock.[41] Southern's modified scheme was opposed by a shareholders' committee but was approved by the Corporation on 26 August 1903 and embodied in the Manchester Ship Canal (Finance) Act, which became law on 22 July 1904.[42]

The Act of 1904 established relations between the Company and the Corporation on a new and permanent basis. It secured to the City of Manchester a permanent predominance in the administration of the Company by making the £5 million debentures perpetual and linking the destinies of Company and City together for ever. In return the Corporation reduced its claim for arrears to the actual outlay incurred in interest and expenses, reducing the amount of arrears by 46 per cent from £1,869,701 to £1,015,209, writing off the balance and funding the remainder. In satisfaction of that debt it accepted 3½ per cent non-cumulative preference shares which ranked for dividend after the debentures but before the old preference shares, so becoming in effect pre-preference shares. It also reduced the rate of interest on its debentures by 29 per cent from 4½ per cent to 3½ per cent. The agreement relieved the ratepayers from future contributions to the rates estimated at £255,550 during the five years 1905–09;[43] it enabled the Company to meet its Corporation debenture obligations in full from 1910, when the Corporation dissolved the special Ship Canal Committee established in 1891. The Act of 1904 permitted the Company to borrow another £2 million which would take priority over the £5 million of Corporation debentures and would be used for the works essential to bring the traffic necessary for profits and dividends. It also benefited the preference shareholders and enabled them to convert their shares into perpetual debentures similar to those of the Corporation, at the price of conceding a third of their potential dividends to the ordinary

[41] Manchester Corporation, *Report of the Ship Canal Committee*, 29 September 1903, 1–13, J. W. Southern.

[42] B.O.D., 350–2, 6 November 1903. Manchester Ship Canal Company, *Report of the Directors*, 18 February 1904, 1–6.

[43] Manchester Corporation, *Report of the Ship Canal Committee*, 7 August 1903, 2, J. W. Southern.

shareholders.[44] Above all, it improved the ultimate prospects of the ordinary shareholders by removing a colossal and constantly increasing burden of debt.

The financial reorganisation of 1904 established very close relations between Corporation and Company but left the actual administration of the Canal in the hands of the Company. Two Corporation directors inspired sufficient trust in their capacity to secure election as shareholders' directors. A succession of able deputy chairmen were recruited in the persons of Alderman J. W. Southern (1897–1908), Sir William Henry Vaudrey (1908–14) and Alderman William Kay (1919–55). That *entente cordiale* made possible the successive election to the board of directors of the first Labour councillor in 1916,[45] a woman alderman in 1964 and the first Labour deputy chairman in 1971.

Through the Canal Company the Corporation of Manchester extended its influence along the flood plain of the Mersey and thereby presented a challenge to other local authorities. It survived several attempts to convert the Company into a public trust representative of the whole region[46] but it could not enforce its authority without trammel throughout the legal limits of the Port of Manchester. Thus it had to accept minority representation upon the Mersey and Irwell Joint Committee, which was created in 1891[47] and which became a vehicle for complaints of pollution during summer droughts from 1896. It was also saddled with a Port Sanitary Authority which was created in 1896 at the original initiative of Salford.[48]

[44] B.O.D., 121, 5 May 1905; 128–9, 12 May; 136–7, 29 May; 141, 9 June 1905.

[45] *Manchester Guardian*, 26 October 1916, 3i–ii; 11 August 1934, 14iii–iv, on Councillor Tom Fox (1860–1934).

[46] *Manchester City News*, 23 July 1892, 5iii–iv; 30 July, 5ii–iii; 6 August, 5ii–iii; 13 August, 8iv–vi; 16 June 1894, 4vii; 18 August, 5iii–v; 25 August, 5i–ii; 28 August 1897, 5iv–v. *Northern Finance and Trade*, 1 December 1897, 456; 8 December, 467.

[47] B.O.D., 266, 22 November 1889; 400–1, 4 December 1891; 374–5, 15 September 1893.

[48] Salford Corporation, *Minutes of Special Committees*, vol. 2, 2 December 1893, 346, S. Brown, Town Clerk.

In its relations with local authorities, such as Salford and Warrington, the Canal Company was fortified by the strength of its statutory position, by the best of legal advice and, above all, by the powerful support of the Corporation directors. The neighbouring town of Salford had provided the land for the docks which Manchester lacked. Its corporation had agreed to a postponement of the construction of Ordsall Dock, No. 5,[49] but had been offended by its exclusion from the loans of 1891–93 and by the consequent denial of direct representation upon the board of directors. Salford also feared competition with its cattle market, the largest in England, from the import of foreign cattle to the Foreign Animals Wharf projected at Mode Wheel. The borough became, however, an immediate and major beneficiary by the increase in its ratable value and twice, in 1896 and 1899, considered aiding the Canal Company to extend its terminal facilities in order to retain trade on its side of the docks. Salford increased its population almost twice as fast as Manchester during the 1890s. The rapid expansion of building and settlement to the west of the historic town first filled up the district along the north bank of the Ship Canal from Ordsall to Weaste and then extended from Windsor Bridge along the roads to Eccles and Bolton, engulfing the exclusive bowery suburb of Pendleton.

Warrington failed to extend its boundaries in 1890 and 1895 to include part of the Ship Canal or to become an entrepôt by means of the Lancashire Derbyshire & East Coast Railway proposed in 1890–91. It was much more affected, however, by the fundamental change in the regime of the Mersey. The river had been used by local traders for navigation and for manufacturing purposes but suffered a loss in volume to the Ship Canal of some 70 per cent instead of the statutory 10 per cent.[50] An agreement of 9 April 1896 relieved the Company of its obligation to construct a dock at Warrington in return for a deep-water wharf and reduced the tolls paid by local traders by 25 per cent on cargo in vessels up to 250 tons using Walton Lock and Eastham

49 T.L.P.C., 44–5, 9 March 1892.

50 *Fairclough & Sons v. The Manchester Ship Canal Company in the Supreme Court of Judicature, Court of Appeal, 25 November 1896–21 January 1897*, 138–9, L. J. Lindley, Lord Chief Justice.

Locks but reaffirmed the Company's obligation to dredge the river for some two and a half miles.[51] The Company's failure after 1898 to perform that onerous task led the traders of Warrington to wage a successful five-year legal battle (1902–07).[52] The Company remained burdened with the high cost of dredging and could not secure, even in 1960, any statutory relief.

The history of the Canal as an operating enterprise is as heroic a tale as that of its construction. The initial obstacles to its use proved immense and unanticipated. The challenge they presented to the administration of the Company was constantly renewed. To respond to those challenges was the achievement of four distinguished chairmen, who remained in office for an average of eighteen and a half years each and two of whom died in harness. Those four allied to a fine commercial sense the organising capacity of generals and they acquired a quasi-monarchical prestige.

John Kenworthy Bythell (1840–1916)[53] was a Manchester Scot who joined the mercantile firm of Gaddum & Co., was attracted to Bombay in 1864 by the great wartime boom in cotton and served as the firm's resident partner in the city for nearly twenty years. He initiated in 1867 and carried through against powerful opposition the construction of the harbour works of the city. Elected chairman of the Bombay Chamber of Commerce in 1872, he led the movement to transfer the administration of the new harbour from the Public Works Department to the Bombay Port Trust and became one of its first members in 1873, so introducing the mercantile element into the management of the port. He retained his interest in India after returning to Manchester and defended the Government of India

[51] B.O.D., 360, 5 July 1895; 388, 16 August; 422–3, 11 October; 86, 10 April 1896.

[52] Ibid., 50, 14 March 1902; 237–8, 17 April 1903; 433–4, 3 May 1907; 7, 2 August 1907.

[53] *Manchester Faces and Places*, vol. 10:4, January 1894, 56–7. *Salford Chronicle*, 18 August 1894, 5i–ii. *Northern Finance and Trade*, 2 February 1898, 90–1. *Manchester Guardian*, 19 August 1916, 6i–ii, 9i. *Manchester City News*, 19 August 1916, 6iii–iv.

against its nationalist critics, advocating the extension of railways by means of government loans and the reduction of railway rates in the interest of the people of India.[54] In Manchester he became one of the twenty-three founder-members of the Ship Canal Consultative Committee in 1886 and, after the resignation of Daniel Adamson (1818–90) as chairman, a director of the Canal Company in 1887. On the same day that he joined the board, Bythell became chairman of the Finance Committee.[55] From 1891 he served as one of the three shareholders' directors on the seven-member executive committee which under Harwood's chairmanship completed the construction of the great enterprise. From 1892 he served as chairman of the Traffic and Rates Committee, 'the most important Committee of the Board'.[56] In 1893 he served for four critical months as acting deputy chairman in place of J.C. Lee (1832–95), the head of Tootal's, and negotiated the second loan from the Corporation.[57] His exhaustive report of 30 May 1894 on the traffic of the Canal was the first such survey made and the first to be published:[58] it ensured his election as chairman of the board in succession to Lord Egerton of Tatton (1832–1909). Lord Rothschild had recommended on 12 June in the interests of the preference shareholders that the Company should have a full-time 'responsible head' or manager at an annual salary of £3,000 and the Ship Canal Committee of the Corporation insisted upon the appointment of Bythell.[59] His election on 20 July 1894 ushered in a new era in the history of the Canal Company.

Bythell became the first paid and resident chairman in the history of the Company and wound up his connection with his cotton firm in order to devote himself entirely to his new charge. Assuming office

[54] J. K. Bythell, 'Railways in India: their Advantages and the Necessity for their Extension', *Journal of the Manchester Geographical Society*, 2 March 1887, 26–41, reprinted (Manchester, Guardian Printing Works, 1887, 22 pp.).

[55] B.O.D., 457, 460, 10 February 1887.

[56] T.L.P.C., 67, 13 May 1892; 128, 28 October 1892; 19, 12 June 1893. T.R.C., 73, 25 May 1894.

[57] B.O.D., 201–2, 6 February 1893; 285–96, 12 June 1893.

[58] Ibid., 87–97, 8 June 1894, reprinted in *Manchester Guardian*, 9 June 1894, 9ii–v.

[59] B.O.D., 103–4, 22 June 1894; 107–10, 6 July; 111–17, 20 July 1894.

at a critical juncture in the affairs of the Canal,[60] he was invested with complete power as both managing director and chairman and he became 'the second founder of the Manchester Ship Canal'.[61] Unrivalled in the strength of his intellect, character and constitution, he proved to be a skilful diplomat as well as a second Adamson in his vigorous defence of the Company against all opponents.[62] He maintained harmonious relations between the Corporation directors and the shareholders' directors, persuaded the Corporation to allow its interest to fall into arrears and established a permanent partnership between Corporation and Company in 1904. He secured the services of a fellow Anglo-Indian, Sir Edward Jenkinson, as chairman of the Finance Committee for twenty years from 1894. He recruited the very ablest directors to represent the interests of the shareholders, including in 1904 Sir Frank Forbes Adam (1846–1926), chairman of the Bombay Chamber of Commerce (1883–89) and president of the Manchester Chamber of Commerce in 1894 and 1904, and in 1906 Allan Hughes (1853–1928), chairman of the Federal Steam Navigation Company. Above all, he supplied the driving energy necessary to attract and retain traffic. 'Trade cannot be diverted from accustomed routes and traders will not change their modes of working in a day. Constant work, time and patience are required to bring traffic from an old to a new centre and the delay should cause no discouragement, no apprehension as to the ultimate success of the endeavour to develope a large and paying traffic.'[63]

The quest for profitable traffic was the supreme aim governing his administration in all its aspects, in the regulation of tolls, in the creation of a 'promotional tariff',[64] in the creation of dockside facilities, in the establishment of rail links with Trafford Park, in the disposal of canalside land, in the sponsorship of trade associations and in the

[60] *Manchester City News*, 26 May 1894, 5ii–v, Joseph Lawrence, 'Thoughts on Board the Skirmisher. A Do-Nothing Canal Policy Spells Ruin'. Ibid., 9 June 1894, 5vii–6i–ii, idem, 'Ship Canal Management and Policy'.

[61] *Manchester Guardian*, 19 August 1916, 6i, 9i.

[62] *Manchester City News*, 1 September 1894, 4vi, 'The Ship Canal's New Aggressive Policy'.

[63] B.O.D., 90, 8 June 1894; 175, 19 October 1894.

[64] T.R.C., 56–7, 2 August 1894; B.O.D., 176, 19 October 1894.

choice of fellow directors. In order to draw the import and export trade of Lancashire's staple industry through the new port he encouraged the establishment in 1894 of the Manchester Cotton Association, becoming its vice-president, and secured the conclusion of the crucial contract of 29 December 1894 for the shipment of piece-goods direct from Manchester to Bombay. He enlisted the support of a number of wealthy 'friends of the Canal' to provide the port through the leasing system with warehouses and a new dock. He weathered the crisis in share prices of 1897–98[65] and assumed the initiative in the establishment of Manchester Liners Ltd in 1898. He created the tradition of the chairman as monarch of the Canal,[66] managed shareholders' meetings with the same efficiency as the undertaking itself and maintained the deep-rooted faith of the small investor in the future of the enterprise. 'I say that we are laying the foundations of a colossal trade which will eventually make Manchester one of the foremost ports in the kingdom.'[67] By 1903 he had made Manchester into the fourth largest importing port of the U.K. and continued to plan for even more prospective traffic. He secured the execution of four successive programmes of improvement works, beginning with the four-year plan of 1897 and culminating in the construction (1902–05) of No. 9 Dock on the site of the former racecourse. The new dock was opened by King Edward VII on 13 July 1905[68] and, coupled with the deepening of the Canal from 26 ft to 28 ft (1905–08), made Manchester into a great railway port in sharp contrast to Liverpool. Bythell inspired the foundation in 1908 of the Manchester Association of Importers and Exporters in order to aid in the development of the port[69] and became its vice-chairman, reporting in confidence that the Canal could in the event of war

[65] *Northern Finance and Trade*, 6 October 1897, 276; 1 December 1897, 456; 8 December 1897, 467; 23 February 1898, 148.

[66] *Manchester City News*, 19 August 1916, 6iv.

[67] Manchester Ship Canal Company, *Report of the Directors*, 11 August 1898, 10, J. K. Bythell.

[68] B.O.D., 150, 14 July 1905; 154–5, 28 July 1905. *The Engineer*, 28 July 1905, 88, 94.

[69] Manchester Cotton Association, *Minutes of the Board*, 91, 10 July 1907, J. K. Bythell. B.O.D., 473, 12 July 1907.

increase its tonnage fivefold.[70] He organised the publicity campaign of 1910 and focused its efforts around the slogan 'Manchester Goods for Manchester Docks'.[71] He did not achieve all his aims and in particular did not secure the planned No. 10 Dock,[72] but he became the true founder of the Port of Manchester, translating a legal concept into a commercial reality. He guided the destinies of the Canal Company for twenty-two years while all the rest of the directors save one changed. He retained the support of his loyal shareholders against a small band of dissidents at the annual meetings in 1915 and 1916.[73] He crowned his career by paying a first dividend to the ordinary shareholder for the year 1915, thirty years after the foundation of the Company. Shunning all personal publicity, he excluded his name from *Who's Who*, declined all national honours and never became a public figure. His memorial survives in the modern ports of Bombay and Manchester.

The successor of J. K. Bythell was William Charles Frederick Bacon (1855–1931),[74] who came from a long line of seafarers, went to sea at the age of fifteen and commanded his first sailing vessel at the age of twenty-two in 1877. When Captain Bacon retired from the sea in 1884 he established the firm of Sivewright Bacon & Co. as shipping brokers in West Hartlepool. On the opening of the Manchester Ship Canal he began operations in Manchester, expanded into ship owning and founded in 1894 the Manchester Bombay & General Navigation Co. Ltd, a precursor of Manchester Liners, and in 1898 the Manchester & Salford Steamship Co. Ltd for services to Virginia and Carolina for the carriage of cattle, cotton and tobacco. He became the first ship owner to be elected to the board of directors of the Canal Company in 1902.[75] As the successor of

[70] Manchester Association of Importers and Exporters, *Minutes*, 48–50, 15 June 1910, J. K. Bythell to Colonel H. Stansbury, R.N.

[71] B.O.D., 374, 4 March 1910; 399–400, 27 May; 440, 16 September; 42, 3 March 1911.

[72] *Manchester Guardian*, 23 June 1900, 6ii. B.O.D., 446–9, 12 March 1913.

[73] *Manchester City News*, 30 January 1915, 4, 6, until 3 April 1915, 6iv; 18 December 1915, 7iv; 15 January 1916, 4iv–v; 26 February 1916, 5i–ii.

[74] *Manchester Guardian*, 13 January 1931, 6iii–v.

[75] B.O.D., 95, 4 July 1902; 128, 12 September 1902.

Chairmen of the Manchester Ship Canal Company, 1916–71 (*Manchester Ship Canal Company*).
Captain William C. Bacon, 1916–31 (*above left*).
Sir Frederick J. West, C.B.E., 1933–50 (*above, right*).
Sir Leslie Roberts, C.B.E., 1950–71 (*left*).

Bythell from 1916 to 1931 he was the only qualified sea captain to preside over the destinies of the Canal, and he strengthened the alliance with Manchester Liners. Most of all he wished to see the Canal pay its own way and he transformed the Company into a permanent payer of dividends, which continued even during the severest depression in its history, in 1921. Manchester extended the range of its influence by means of both steamships and motor lorries and maintained its position as the fourth largest port, measured by the value of its imports and exports, from 1906 to 1930. The central position acquired by the Canal in the business life of the city was symbolised by the new Ship Canal House opened in 1927.[76] Under Captain Bacon the port opened its first oil dock in 1922 and the balance of its activity began to tilt westwards towards the 'stony hill' of Stanlow.

Sir Frederick J. West (1872–1959)[77] was the second native Mancunian to serve as chairman in succession to Alfred Watkin (1858–1947),[78] who held office in 1931–33. F.J. West was the first chairman recruited by the Company from the City Council and its most distinguished chairman since the time of Lord Egerton (1887–94). He spent his business life in the gas industry as the head of West's Gas Improvement Company, which had been founded by his father in 1874 under the spur of the 'coal famine'.[79] He became a Conservative city councillor in 1905, an alderman in 1920 and lord mayor in 1924–25. He became a Corporation director of the Canal Company in 1917 and its chairman at the age of sixty-one in 1933, resigning from the City Council in order to secure election as a shareholders' director. West assumed office after the world depression of 1929–32 had reduced the ordinary dividend to ½ per cent for the year 1932. He maintained good relations with the Company's employees, especially the dockers, during a long period of stag-

[76] *Manchester Guardian*, 8 November 1927, 14vii; 12 November, 12ii. *Supplement to the Manchester Guardian*, 13 December 1927, 30, 'New Headquarters of the Ship Canal Company. Sky-scraping comes to Manchester'.

[77] Ibid., 16 November 1959, 14iii.

[78] Ibid., 21 July 1947, 6v.

[79] Ibid., 14 January 1922, 11v, on John West (1839–1922), his father.

nation in traffic when the competition of Liverpool became acute after the opening of the East Lancashire Road in 1933.[80] So profound was the economic depression that West came to believe in the impotence of any port authority to command traffic.[81] He became president-elect of the Manchester Chamber of Commerce in 1934 but declined to serve because of the pressure of business.[82] He did, however, supply the Port of Manchester Committee established by the Chamber in 1935 with its first and most effective chairman. He also became the first chairman to be knighted, in 1936, the first to serve on the board of Manchester Liners (1942–55) and the first to write his memoirs.[83]

Leslie Roberts (1896–1976)[84] was recruited into the service of the Company as the heir apparent to Sir Frederick West. He served as chairman from 1950 to 1971, or for almost as long a period as Bythell, supplying shrewd and compelling leadership to the Company during the most prosperous era in its history. He spent all his life in shipping, becoming general manager of Frederick Leyland & Co. Ltd (1929–34) and moving from Liverpool to Manchester in 1934. He became general manager of the Canal Company in 1936 and held that most strenuous of posts for a full decade, serving during the war of 1939–45 as chairman of the Port Emergency Committee and therefore as supreme commander of all port operations. At the end of the war he became managing director in 1945 and, after only five years on the board, chairman in 1950, combining the function of managing director with that of chairman until 1961. He was knighted in 1952 and presided over the transfer of the port's traffic connections from rail to road in the 1950s, over the oil boom which carried tonnage to an all-time peak in 1959 and over the beginning of

80 Ibid., 28 April 1933, 11i–ii. Manchester Cotton Association, *Minutes of the Board*, 6–7, 12 January 1937.

81 Manchester Ship Canal Company, *Report of the Directors*, 25 February 1935, 5.

82 Manchester Chamber of Commerce, *Monthly Record*, 28 February 1935, 40.

83 F. J. West, *Reflections and Reminiscences* (Manchester, West's Gas Improvement Co., 1948), 82–8, 'Municipal Experiences'.

84 *The Times*, 29 June 1976, 16viii.

the container revolution in cargo handling in 1966. He raised dividends to levels without precedent from 1963 and retired in 1971, remaining a director of Manchester Liners from 1947 to 1975 and becoming the first honorary president of the Canal Company for the last five years of his life.

Table 1

Trade of the ports of Manchester and Liverpool, 1894–1976

	Value of the trade of Manchester (£)		*Proportion of trade of U.K. of Manchester and Liverpool (%)*					
	Imports	*Domestic exports*	*Imports*		*Domestic exports*		*Re-exports*	
Year			*M*	*L*	*M*	*L*	*M*	*L*
1894	2,790,129	4,019,344	0·7	23·3	1·9	36·2	0·2	18·1
1895	4,220,792	8,836,999	1·0	22·9	3·9	34·6	0·3	20·9
1896	7,732,416	8,338,447	1·8	23·4	3·5	34·1	0·5	20·4
1897	8,311,878	7,408,430	1·8	22·6	3·2	32·9	0·5	22·5
1898	9,163,977	7,933,542	2·0	23·6	3·4	32·1	0·5	21·8
1899	10,714,369	8,609,516	2·2	22·7	3·3	30·7	0·5	24·7
1900	16,159,954	7,416,873	3·1	23·8	2·5	30·0	0·7	23·9
1901	14,901,401	7,929,148	2·9	25·2	2·8	32·2	0·5	23·2
1902	17,620,772	8,001,563	3·3	24·1	2·8	32·2	0·5	26·8
1903	20,279,255	8,856,100	3·8	23·8	3·1	32·9	0·7	27·2
1904	21,468,225	10,869,790	3·9	25·0	3·6	35·6	1·5	25·4
1905	23,290,796	11,956,514	4·1	24·7	3·6	35·7	2·1	26·5
1906	26,536,274	12,920,812	4·4	24·1	3·4	34·5	1·6	24·4
1907	30,402,229	15,754,398	4·7	24·8	3·7	33·6	1·2	25·0
1908	25,647,640	14,498,684	4·3	23·7	3·8	32·4	0·3	24·9
1909	28,943,444	14,315,329	4·6	23·8	3·8	33·2	0·3	26·4
1910	29,944,905	17,277,429	4·4	25·1	4·0	32·8	0·2	28·3
1911	32,502,954	21,375,265	4·8	23·5	4·7	32·9	0·3	26·5
1912	35,111,128	21,182,625	4·7	24·1	4·4	33·6	0·4	27·2
1913	35,290,606	20,630,339	4·6	22·8	4·0	32·4	0·3	23·0
1914	33,741,734	18,806,298	4·8	23·9	4·4	34·4	0·4	24·9

	Value of the trade of Manchester (£)		*Proportion of trade of U.K. of Manchester and Liverpool (%)*					
	Imports	*Domestic exports*	*Imports*		*Domestic exports*		*Re-exports*	
Year			*M*	*L*	*M*	*L*	*M*	*L*
1915	39,656,092	16,678,988	4·7	27·0	4·3	34·9	0·3	28·9
1916	47,967,835	20,892,794	5·1	29·5	4·1	33·4	1·3	27·5
1917	57,731,668	29,555,198	5·4	35·0	5·6	38·8	1·9	28·2
1918	78,193,280	28,271,391	5·9	36·8	5·6	38·3	2·0	20·9
1919	98,308,318	45,209,335	6·0	33·8	5·7	29·4	2·0	26·1
1920	137,798,806	62,208,306	7·1	28·3	4·7	36·0	3·5	28·9
1921	51,872,821	33,592,546	4·8	22·2	4·8	37·3	1·0	22·4
1922	51,826,584	39,159,041	5·2	22·2	5·4	33·8	1·0	17·4
1923	55,947,658	36,422,912	5·1	22·2	4·7	34·8	1·5	18·9
1924	72,804,516	40,277,790	5·7	22·0	5·0	34·1	1·1	20·6
1925	71,865,119	42,839,980	5·4	21·7	5·5	34·3	0·6	18·3
1926	64,855,720	30,536,168	5·2	19·8	4·7	36·7	0·8	17·9
1927	60,295,244	33,315,871	4·9	18·3	4·7	33·8	0·7	15·5
1928	65,643,243	32,316,343	5·5	19·3	4·5	32·9	0·4	13·7
1929	68,889,303	30,395,699	5·6	18·9	4·2	31·6	0·6	15·1
1930	55,227,853	20,365,831	5·3	16·5	3·6	29·2	0·8	14·0
1931	40,649,638	13,934,013	4·7	15·3	3·6	26·9	0·8	11·2
1932	35,334,833	12,809,169	5·0	17·8	3·5	29·0	0·8	12·8
1933	35,522,553	10,914,630	5·3	18·3	3·0	29·2	0·7	12·2
1934	38,651,705	11,074,936	5·3	18·7	2·8	29·0	0·6	13·1
1935	39,767,157	12,758,054	5·3	18·6	3·0	29·5	0·7	11·8
1936	45,542,582	13,322,256	5·4	18·8	3·0	29·6	0·5	13·0
1937	56,396,491	15,029,505	5·5	18·9	2·9	29·8	0·5	15·7
1938	44,956,475	12,436,821	4·9	17·7	2·7	28·1	0·5	10·7
1939	47,071,963	13,169,273	5·3	20·8	3·0	30·2	0·9	13·4
1946	59,890,075	45,422,882	4·6	30·3	5·0	34·6	3·1	32·6
1947	102,808,761	58,552,115	5·7	26·5	5·1	33·9	2·6	31·4
1948	138,642,377	69,370,245	6·7	26·3	4·4	33·7	1·1	19·2
1949	147,425,647	70,774,942	6·5	24·8	4·0	33·4	2·8	18·7
1950	173,367,230	90,959,182	6·7	24·2	4·2	30·6	1·3	18·6
1951	269,459,849	89,905,045	6·9	23·2	3·5	30·5	1·3	15·3

	Value of the trade of Manchester (£)		*Proportion of trade of U.K. of Manchester and Liverpool (%)*					
	Imports	*Domestic exports*	*Imports*		*Domestic exports*		*Re-exports*	
Year			*M*	*L*	*M*	*L*	*M*	*L*
1952	219,882,753	90,517,645	6·3	21·9	3·5	31·0	0·8	25·5
1953	189,596,470	99,928,646	5·7	21·4	3·9	28·9	1·0	16·6
1954	237,420,453	101,459,008	7·1	20·0	3·8	28·9	0·6	12·9
1955	258,993,814	105,382,907	6·7	19·1	3·7	26·5	0·8	15·6
1956	277,765,102	128,546,659	7·2	19·3	4·1	27·8	1·3	22·9
1957	287,940,828	122,988,469	7·1	19·2	3·7	27·8	0·9	15·9
1958	251,175,496	121,792,206	6·7	17·9	3·8	27·8	0·7	21·1
1959	247,670,248	122,782,586	6·2	17·7	3·7	27·0	1·3	16·2
1960	285,164,062	127,898,357	6·3	17·8	3·6	26·0	0·7	18·3
1961	235,780,340	113,642,013	5·4	18·4	3·1	25·1	0·7	16·8
1962	228,750,174	127,324,052	5·1	17·3	3·4	23·2	0·7	14·0
1963	252,436,707	125,145,620	5·2	17·2	3·1	22·7	0·6	10·4
1964	286,223,791	131,966,043	5·2	16·9	3·1	22·8	0·8	10·3
1965	286,656,015	143,390,396	5·0	16·3	3·0	21·2	0·9	10·7
1966	282,357,403	127,605,444	4·8	15·7	2·8	19·8	1·1	7·9
1967	301,061,530	147,730,307	4·7	13·9	2·9	18·1	0·6	7·5
1968	347,631,699	200,659,033	4·4	13·1	3·2	17·0	0·9	8·2
1969	346,895,217	211,014,607	4·2	12·5	3·0	16·0	1·1	8·2
1970	411,247,428	210,171,304	4·6	11·4	2·6	14·9		
1971	394,640,436	280,694,104	4·0	10·5	3·0	14·6		
1972	421,818,172	304,343,670	3·8	8·5	3·1	9·7		
1973	567,559,030	364,151,737	3·6	6·8	2·9	9·5		
1974	769,809,535	491,864,495	3·3	7·2	3·0	8·4		
1975	682,157,769	466,879,776	2·8	7·2	2·4	9·2		
1976	962,576,730	660,420,112	3·1	6·3	2·7	9·0		

Source: Annual Statements of the Trade of the U.K., 1894–1974. Re-exports from the port of Manchester reached a significant level only during the years 1904–07 and 1916–27 and have been included only in the second part of the table. From 1970 they were not recorded separately from domestic exports for individual ports.

2

The establishment of the Montreal–Manchester axis by Manchester Liners

The Ship Canal was no mere waterway but a symbolic declaration of economic independence by Manchester and an instrument of commercial revolution designed to undermine the whole complex of interests vested in a main artery of transport, turning against Liverpool the techniques whereby it had captured the trade of the Midlands from Bristol. As such it represented the greatest challenge ever made to the established interests and the corporate pride of the business community of Lancashire's leading city. That port was wholly dependent upon its function as a non-industrial entrepôt between the outer world and its manufacturing hinterland. It had suffered since the 1840s a reduction in its large share of the trade of the U.K. through the competition of Glasgow, Cardiff and London and it had lost to Hamburg during the decade 1885–95 its position as the first port of Europe. Its mercantile élite had initiated almost every improvement in transport facilities extending its hinterland and had inevitably acquired a deep-rooted corporate pride in their port and their river. That élite was determined to deny any ocean shipping to the new artery and so to reduce it to a mere barge canal. They sought to achieve their end through the shipping conference, establishing five such associations between 1893 and 1897, and through the deferred rebate, whose use they extended from 1895.

The Ship Canal was primarily designed to link the Lancashire cotton industry to its markets in Asia, especially India and China, by a waterway dug to the same depth as the Suez Canal. 'The growth of the Suez Canal is in a very great measure synonymous with the growth of the Lancashire and adjacent manufacturing districts.'[1] The Ship Canal did, however, attract coasting vessels to Runcorn and Pomona as well as a large short-sea trade to Europe. In the coasting trade outward freights were reduced from 1894 by 25 per cent to Glasgow and by 35 per cent to London at the expense of the railways rather than of the shipping lines. In the short-sea trade services were begun in 1894 to the Baltic, to France and to Spain: the agents for those services formed in 1894 the Manchester Steamship Lines Association in order to negotiate more effectively with shippers, importers and the Ship Canal Company.[2] In the deep-sea trades the establishment of permanent connections proved much more difficult. Services were, however, begun to the cotton ports of the U.S.A., to Egypt and to Brazil in 1894, to Bombay and to the Persian Gulf in 1895, to the Black Sea in 1897, to Canada in 1898, to the West Indies in 1902–11, to Australia in 1904 and to New Zealand in 1906. All the early attempts failed to develop regular services to Denmark, the Adriatic, Turkey, Bengal, Ceylon, Java, China or to North, West and South Africa.[3] The greatest difficulty of all was experienced in trying to gain entry to the main American trades, to the Argentine, to Chile and, above all, to New York. Only the two world wars reduced the opposition of ship owners to serving the new port: thereafter services were established to Calcutta in 1920 and to South Africa in 1924, to the West Indies in 1947 and from West Africa in 1958.

The opening of the Canal in an era of commercial depression did not reproduce the immediate success of the Liverpool–Manchester railway of 1830. It revealed a weakness in economic theory whereby 'of course a superior route asserts its own superiority automatically.'[4] It proved that a thriving port required more than docks and access to

[1] Manchester Ship Canal, *Description of the Project Now Before Parliament, and Exposition of its Objects, Commercial Advantages and Financial Prospects* (Manchester, Provisional Committee, 1884), 49.

[2] T.R.C., 59–60, 8 February 1894.

[3] *Manchester Guardian*, 17 November 1897, 11iii, 'Manchester and South Africa. Proposed Steamship Service'.

[4] Ibid., 29 August 1894, 5iii.

the sea: it ushered in an era of conferences, associations and schemes designed to divert traffic to the new route and to overcome the opposition of both railways and ship owners. The railway companies acted as a solid phalanx in defence of their interests, declining to offer any advantage to a rival undertaking which would shorten their mileage and reduce their rates of carriage. They had acquired a large vested interest in the transport of overseas goods from the London market. They delayed completing the main link to the Salford docks until 1898 and they did not establish their own wharves in the port, as railroad companies did in the U.S.A., but built new goods stations outside the dock area. For six long years until 1897 they delayed conceding the vital exceptional rates which were granted at ports on such articles as grain, timber and cotton carried in great bulk and weight and which were applicable to most of the traffic of the Canal.[5] They prevented the Ship Canal from generating new traffic for all the inland navigations connected with it and controlled by the railways. They retained control of the home trade and of its extension in the trade with Ireland.[6]

Liverpool and London remained the ports most hostile to the development of the Canal's hinterland, London excluding Manchester from the Australasian trade, Liverpool debarring it from the American trade and both denying it access to the trade to Africa and Asia. The Mersey Docks & Harbour Board was galvanised into unprecedented activity by the threat of competition: it dredged away the Mersey bar between 1890 and 1894 and extended accommodation for the trades in cattle, wool and timber threatened by the competition of Manchester. Liverpool merchants opened branches in Manchester in order to retain control over the import of timber, grain and cotton. They also founded the Manchester & Liverpool Transport Co. Ltd (1898–1910) for the transit trade. They favoured

[5] B.O.D., 269–70, 18 June 1897.

[6] *Manchester Guardian*, 7 February 1901, 8i, 'A Ship Canal Traffic Plan'. *The Manchester Ship Canal, and How to Make it Pay a Dividend. The 'Robert Jones' Scheme*, (Manchester, Sherratt, 1902, 24 pp.). *Manchester Guardian*, 10 February 1898, 10i–ii; 14 February, 10ii–iii; 16 February, 12iii–iv; 23 February, 10iv–v, 'Ireland and the Ship Canal'.

projects for the development of transport by road, light railway and even electric express railway (1901–03) in order to maintain the hinterland of their port, even at the expense of the railway companies.[7] Local ship owners competed out of existence an experimental line established from Manchester to West Africa in 1895–96[8] and prevented the launch in 1895 of an independent service from Manchester to the Levant. Liverpool retained without any fear of challenge its passenger and emigrant traffic and its express goods traffic, remaining the last port of call for vessels leaving Manchester. From 1899 it expanded its re-export trade and so developed the one branch of commerce which its inland rival was least adapted to handle. The mere increment in the value of its imports between 1894 and 1913 amounted to almost treble the value of Manchester's total imports in 1913, while the increment in the value of its exports was more than four times the value of all Manchester's exports in 1913. Its implacable opposition compelled Manchester to turn, until 1934, to the ports of the north-east coast for aid in the development of its shipping services.

The continued opposition of Liverpool to attempts to divert its traffic convinced Bythell that Manchester required its own shipping line as an essential corollary to its Ship Canal. He was fortified in that conclusion by the failure of successive efforts by friendly ship owners to establish a regular and permanent line to North America. The Canada & Newfoundland Steamship Company could not secure enough return cargo from Manchester.[9] Christopher Furness (1852–1912), who had established his own shipping firm at West Hartlepool in 1882 and had formed Furness Withy & Co. Ltd in 1891, failed in 1895 to buy the necessary steamers for a Canadian service and was thus frustrated in his earliest efforts to establish a separate line

[7] *Manchester City News*, 26 September 1896, 5vi; 17 October, 6iv; 28 December, 6v–vi. *Manchester Guardian*, 23 October 1896, 7vii.

[8] B.O.D., 352, 21 June 1895. P. N. Davies, *The Trade Makers. Elder Dempster in West Africa 1852–1972* (London, Allen, 1973), 104–7.

[9] B.O.D., 255–6, 15 February 1895; 283, 22 March 1895.

[10] Ibid., 316, 26 April 1895; 333, 24 May 1895.

from Manchester.[10] The Manchester Bombay & General Navigation Company under Captain Bacon began a service between Montreal and Manchester in April 1895 but found that its operations proved uneconomic without a subsidy and had to discharge its cattle in Liverpool because the Manchester lairages were not ready.[11] Bythell proposed in 1896 to form a Manchester Ship Canal Steamship Company with a capital of £600,000, sent Marshall Stevens to America to establish relations with railways free from close connections to Liverpool lines, and began negotiations with Furness to inaugurate steamship lines to both North America and the river Plate.[12] As a result Furness Withy & Co. ran steamers from Montreal to Manchester during the summer of 1897 but found that much more support from Manchester merchants was necessary in order to maintain a viable service.

On 16 June 1897 the Prime Minister of Canada undertook a voyage along the Ship Canal after the first Colonial Conference. Bythell was thereby inspired to begin tripartite negotiations with Furness in London, with Laurier in Ottawa and with the Corporation of Manchester as well as with local mercantile friends of the Canal to establish a subsidised line of steamers to Canada.[13] Furness was sufficiently impressed by the Canal, the new lairages and the grain elevator to agree to establish a line of large first-class steamers with refrigerated chambers and cattle appliances, provided that enough financial support could be secured from Manchester and from the Canadian government.[14] The board of directors decided on 25 February 1898 to send an immediate deputation to Canada to seek a subsidy. Two Corporation directors, Alderman Southern and Sir Bosdin Leech (1836–1912), sailed on 9 March to undertake the necessary negotiations in Ottawa and to reinforce the appeal of the Company by the influence of Manchester Corporation.[15] They

[11] Ibid., 351, 21 June 1895; 372, 19 July 1895; 27, 17 January 1896.
[12] Ibid., 107, 19 June 1896; 218, 26 February 1897.
[13] Ibid., 332, 19 November 1897; 338, 8 December 1897; 342, 17 December 1897.
[14] Ibid., 359, 11 February 1898; 369–70, 25 February 1898.
[15] Ibid., 376–7, 11 March 1898; 393, 6 May 1898.

secured the support of A. G. Blair (1844–1907), Premier of New Brunswick (1883–96) and Minister of Railways since 1896, and of Sydney Arthur Fisher (1850–1921), the Minister of Agriculture and Commerce, who wished to extend the consumption of Canadian produce amongst the great army of consumers in the heart of industrial England. The Canadian Cabinet approved the grant of a subsidy of £8,000 for three years in return for a fortnightly service and the Canadian Parliament ratified the decision on 14 June 1898.[16] The subsidy may not have been as large as had been desired but was accepted as adequate by Furness in London on 24 March, when Bythell brought two years of negotiation to a successful conclusion.

Manchester Liners Ltd was registered on 3 May 1898 and employed as its brokers Lawson & Ormrod, who had marketed the Canal Company's own debentures since 1892. The issued capital was one-third of the nominal capital and comprised £350,000, half in ordinary shares and half in 5 per cent preference shares. Furness held 10,000 of the 17,500 ordinary shares and 2,500 of the 17,500 preference shares, while the Manchester friends of the Canal took up under Bythell's diligent persuasion 20,000 shares, subscribing to the bulk of the preference capital.[17] The new company was denied a quotation on any stock exchange until 1915 because it had not issued the prescribed one-half of its nominal capital. As a joint creation by London and Manchester it recruited its six directors equally from each city. In Manchester were located its registered office and the port of registry for its vessels as well as its base of operations. Furness supplied most of the capital and shouldered the largest risk in subscribing to 57 per cent of the ordinary shares. He was concerned less with the Ship Canal than with the success of a company identified with himself and intended as a source of orders for his shipyards as well as a fief for inheritance by his son. He even proclaimed in a moment of irritation with the Manchester shareholders, 'I am not interested in the Ship Canal,' and asserted that he could have made the Canal a dividend-paying concern by creating in Manchester a

[16] Ibid., 413–14, 15 July 1898; 423, 29 July 1898.

[17] *Northern Finance and Trade*, 13 April 1898, 287; 4 May 1898, 360.

hundred-steamer company with a capital of £4.25 million and so increasing the value of the Canal Company's shares by more than the cost of the ships.[18] To achieve his ends he himself served as chairman of the board and he appointed as managing director one of the ablest of his employees, Robert Burdon Stoker (1859–1919).[19] For its part the Canal Company granted the new line such privileges as exemption from ships' dues and free towage. It was represented on the small board of directors through two of its own directors, Sir Edward Jenkinson (1836–1919)[20] and Alderman Southern, who personified the respective interests of London investors and of Manchester Corporation in the Ship Canal. A third director, W. H. Vaudrey, served the new company as solicitor and trustee for its debenture holders.

The foundation of Manchester Liners proved even more important than that of Trafford Park Estates in 1896 in the development of the new port. It inspired ambitious hopes that Manchester might breed 'a race of shipowners' and eventually rise to the rank of 'a first class ship-owning port'.[21] Sivewright Bacon & Co. were encouraged to begin a complementary Manchester–Virginia line in 1898 and Lamport & Holt to improve in 1899 the New York–Manchester service which they had begun in 1894 as the last leg of a triangular service to Brazil.[22] Liverpool was dismayed by the threat to its largest single import trade[23] and undertook the deepening of its Canada Docks in 1898. The new line began operations with chartered vessels and inaugurated a summer service to the great grain entrepôt of Montreal and a winter service to St John, N.B., and Halifax, N.S. The safe arrival of the *Manchester City* on 16 January 1899 proved

[18] Manchester Liners Ltd, *Shareholders' Minute Book*, i, 10, 1 September 1900.

[19] Manchester Liners Ltd, *Minute Book* (of the Board of Directors), (henceforth cited as 'M.L.B.'), 16, 23 May 1898. *Manchester Guardian*, 4 September 1919, 12vi. *Manchester City News*, 4 September 1919, 10iv.

[20] *The Times*, 4 March 1919, 12v.

[21] Manchester Ship Canal Company, *Report of the Directors*, 11 August 1898, 7; 21 February 1900, 1, J. K. Bythell.

[22] *Manchester Guardian*, 5 April 1894, 6iii; 9 August 1894, 8iii; 20 October 1898, 8vi.

[23] B.O.D., 481, 13 January 1899.

The arrival of the *Manchester City*, 16 January 1899 (*Manchester Liners Ltd*). The first custom-built vessel of Manchester Liners was launched on 27 October 1898 by Sir Raylton Dixon & Co. Ltd of Cleveland Dockyards, Middlesbrough (*The Engineer*, 18 November 1898, 506). The vessel was 461 ft long, 52 ft broad and 41 ft deep, with a gross tonnage of 5,833 and a net register tonnage of 4,686: the triple-expansion engines of 4,000 i.h.p. supplied by the works of Sir Christopher Furness made possible a speed of 12½–13 knots. 'Her four telescoped masts and telescoped funnel gave her that appearance of squatness which has become the peculiar advertisement of Manchester all over the seven seas . . . She was distinguished by her great size from all other ships that have used the Canal . . . Famous at Middlesbrough as the largest ship ever built on the Tees; famous on the Tyne and on the coasts of Wick and Cromartyshire as the steamer that broke her quadrant during a gale in the Pentland Firth and made her way back zigzag fashion into the North Sea without the help of a rudder, only to lose her anchors and be driven ashore in the Firth of Cromarty; famous at St John in New Brunswick as the greatest ship that ever was seen there; famous in Liverpool as a ship built to do that which had often been declared by Liverpool shipowners to be impossible for any vessel of her size; and famous in Manchester as the first ship built for the Manchester Liners, Limited – the first great steamship company identified with the port, – and the biggest steamer by a thousand tons or more that ever attempted to navigate the Manchester Canal' (*Manchester Guardian*, 16 January 1899, 10iii).

The *Manchester City* was described by its Liverpool sea pilot as 'a pilots' robber' because it carried the cargo of three normal steamers but employed only one pilot. With a deadweight tonnage of 8,600 and a draught of 24½ ft, the vessel was escorted by two tugs. It carried on board 450 head of cattle, 150 sheep and 7,500 tons of general cargo, including 67,000 bushels of maize, 39,929 bushels of wheat, 37,117 bushels and 1,500 bags of oats, 11,972 boxes of cheese, 1,416 boxes of butter, 1,084 cases of eggs, 1,250 tierces of lard, 4,600 bags of starch and 6,470 bundles of pulp as well as an assortment of lumber. The cargo and the ship were worth together nearly £100,000. The bulk of the cargo was delivered within carting distance of the docks. The ship sailed for Halifax on 24 January 1899 with 1,500 tons of exports (*Manchester City News*, 28 January 1899, 6vi). As the only vessel of the fleet of Manchester Liners with refrigerating capacity until 1923, the *Manchester City* inaugurated the River Plate service of the company (1904–08) and continued on the Plate service after 1908 to other British ports. It survived the 1914–18 war and was broken up in 1929 after thirty years of service.

that the Canal could be used by a large steamer with a tonnage of 8,500, a length of 461 ft and a draught of 25 ft.[24] Seven thirteen-knot first-class cargo vessels, designed to suit the dimensions of the Canal and fitted with telescopic topmasts, were ordered from yards on the north-east coast and were financed by the issue in 1899 of £300,000 in 4½ per cent debentures.[25] Unfortunately they were delayed in delivery by an engineers' strike, although three were built in Furness's own yards. The line proved unable for the first year of operations fully to maintain its scheduled fortnightly service because its steamers were not built; it received only half the promised subsidy and experienced 'exceptional difficulty' in collecting even that moiety.[26] Then it suffered the conscription of three of its largest vessels to serve as government transports in the South African War and had to refuse an official offer to purchase two.[27] Thus it did not produce the expected immediate and large accession of revenue to the Canal Company because the fleet of nine vessels became one of six. Nor did it lead to the establishment of other steamship lines in Manchester, because of the competitive attraction of government charters during the war and the long post-war depression in freights.[28]

Manchester Liners nevertheless linked the new port of Manchester to the trunk route of the world's shipping industry. It established the connection with the capital of Canada's transport system upon a firm foundation and, in co-operation with the Canadian Pacific Railway, extended the import of grain, timber, wood-pulp, apples and cattle. The import of apples stimulated the supplementary shipment of oranges from Spain and placed the local fruit trade on a solid basis. The import of cattle brought the Corporation's lairages into use and expanded the trade in American produce, 'the best paying class of traffic', at Manchester.[29] The import of provisions such as hams,

24 *Manchester Guardian*, 16 January 1899, 10iii–v; 17 January, 8v.

25 M.L.B., 23–30, 7 June 1898; 66, 11 May 1899; 183–4, 1 March 1902.

26 Ibid., 81, 7 October 1899; 115, 11 August 1900.

27 Ibid., 100, 24 February 1900.

28 D. H. Aldcroft, 'The Depression in British Shipping, 1901–1911', *Journal of Transport History*, May 1965, 14–23.

29 B.O.D., 393, 17 May 1901.

bacon, cheese and butter from America supplied the Canal with a profitable traffic denied to it by Denmark and Ireland: it led to the formation in 1899 of a Wholesale Provision Merchants' Association for the framing of contracts and the settlement of disputes in Manchester without reference to Liverpool. Manchester Liners also developed a second service to the U.S.A., first to New Orleans during the cotton season from 1899 and then to Philadelphia in 1901, in co-operation with the Leyland Line established in 1873 and with a subsidy from the Philadelphia & Reading Railway Company.[30] It decided not to begin a service to New York in competition with Lamport & Holt but strengthened its Canadian connection by extending its service downriver from Montreal to Quebec in 1902 in association with the new Great Northern Railway Company of Quebec. Thus the new line established two main shuttle services across the stormy waters of the North Atlantic. It proved much more successful in the carriage of imports than of exports because of transatlantic tariff barriers. It increased the share of British shipping in Canada's foreign trade and carried the staples of the Canal's traffic in timber, grain and cotton. Its regular reliable and fast services helped to make Manchester a great centre of distribution. It increased the bunkering trade of the Canal by loading its steamers at Partington with all the coal necessary for the round voyage. Not only did the line bring in substantial revenue to the Canal Company but it also paid during its first four years (1899–1903) an average annual dividend of 6 per cent.

The post-war depression of freights proved acute in the North Atlantic trade and reduced returns from the Canadian service, especially after the establishment in 1903 of a competititive service to Liverpool by the Canadian Pacific Railway.[31] The company was forced to pass its dividend for the eight years from 1904 to 1912 as well as to fall into arrears of interest on both the preference shares and the debentures.[32] A joint service to the river Plate was begun in 1904 in association with the Leyland Line and Furness Withy & Co. as well

[30] M.L.B., 77, 9 August 1899; 110, 14 July 1900; 127, 17 November 1900.
[31] Ibid., 224, 25 April 1903; 242, 30 October 1903; 254, 19 March 1904.
[32] Ibid., 233, 8 August 1903.

as with the Central Northern Railway of Argentina. The new service undertook the profitable carriage of frozen meat but was maintained for only four years against the fierce opposition of the river Plate Conference and the lack of support from Manchester shippers, which provoked Furness in 1907 to threaten to remove the steamers from the Port of Manchester. The abandonment of the Plate venture from 1 January 1908[33] enabled the line to double the frequency of its Montreal service from fortnightly to weekly and so tardily to fulfil the original intention of the founders. That regular weekly service enabled the line to secure better service from the Canadian railways and to withstand the ferocious competition offered by tramp steamers. Manchester Liners benefited by the formation of the North Atlantic Conference in 1908, by the increase in exports from the Port of Manchester from 1909 and by the unprecedented boom in Canadian trade, which was induced by the settlement of the prairies and carried the production and export of wheat to a peak in 1928. From 1911 it began to pay off its arrears of interest and from 1912 it resumed the distribution of dividends, so ending the only dividendless phase in its whole history.

The Great War ushered in a new era in the history of Manchester Liners. Its steamers were again pressed into wartime service, first on charter and then, from 21 March 1917, on requisition as German submarines took heavier toll of British shipping than had ever been expected.[34] The tonnage crisis of 1917 brought to an end the line's Canadian subsidy after 31 March 1917.[35] Altogether the company lost ten out of fifteen steamers, including seven during the first eight months of 1917. It had, however, strengthened its links with the U.S.A. by starting a regular joint service from Baltimore to Manchester in 1915[36] and importing large quantities of Virginia tobacco. The financial returns reaped during the war proved substantial. The company's shares were quoted on the Manchester Stock Exchange

33 Ibid., 350, 29 January 1908.
34 Ibid., 118, 11 May 1917.
35 Ibid., 157, 14 April 1916; 196, 11 October 1917; 225, 22 May 1919.
36 Ibid., 136–7, 10 September 1915; 140, 15 November 1915.

from 1915[37] and rose above par. Its growing reserves were invested in liquid form in municipal and government securities so as to provide for the post-war rebuilding of the fleet.[38] The war presented R. B. Stoker with his greatest challenge and raised him to the peak of his career in 1916–18, when the dividends of Manchester Liners reached heights which were to be surpassed only in 1974. On the death of Lord Furness he had become chairman of the board in 1913 because the local directors deemed it necessary to have a chairman resident in Manchester and acceptable to Manchester merchants.[39] Stoker's energy, ability and tact earned him a high reputation in the district. He gauged much more accurately than his fellow directors of the Manchester Chamber of Commerce the intensity of the anti-German swing in opinion against free trade:[40] he became for the two years 1916–18 the first protectionist president of the Chamber in the twentieth century and thereafter Conservative M.P. for Manchester in 1918. He also became a director of the Ship Canal Company in 1916[41] and so strengthened the special relationship between the two companies which was based upon mutual interest and was regularly acknowledged in an annual interchange of compliments between the two chairmen. 'They were the backbone of the business of the port.'[42] The alliance was maintained by the election to the board of Manchester Liners of successive directors of the Canal Company, including S. W. Royse (1912–17), A. Watkin (1914–47), Lord Colwyn (1927–42), F. J. West (1942–55) and Leslie Roberts (1947–75).

Stoker was succeeded as chairman on his death in 1919 by Frederick

37 Ibid., 128, 18 June 1915; 136–7, 10 September 1915.

38 Ibid., 88, 13 February 1914; 130, 18 June 1915.

39 Ibid., 53–55, 31 January 1913.

40 *Manchester Guardian*, 24 February 1916, 10ii–iv, 'Chamber of Commerce and Free Trade. Thirty Directors Resign'. The three remaining directors were R. B. Stoker, J. K. Bythell and T. Walkden. The new board of directors included Captain W. C. Bacon and Marshall Stevens, who had urged the wider representation on the board of the new trades of the district. Manchester Chamber of Commerce, *Monthly Record*, March 1916, 69; April 1916, 105.

41 M.L.B., 165–6, 26 July 1916.

42 Manchester Liners Ltd, *Shareholders' Minute Book*, i, 57–8, 8 October 1924, W. C. Bacon.

W. Lewis (1870–1944),[43] who had been the assistant of Sir Christopher Furness and had become deputy chairman of Furness Withy & Co. in 1914 and chairman in 1919. Lewis transferred the regular meetings of the board of directors from Manchester to London and made his first trip down the Ship Canal only in 1936. Under his guidance the financial position of Manchester Liners was notably strengthened. The repayment of all the debentures by 1921 freed the company from any charges upon its property, gave it full control over the whole fleet and enhanced the security of both ordinary and preference shareholders. Manchester Liners, itself an associate company of Furness Withy & Co., established during the shipping boom of 1920 its own associate company, Manchester Ocean Services Ltd (1920–30), to acquire three more vessels.[44] From 1920 it invested in the Economic Insurance Company, in order to share in the marine insurance of its own ships.[45] From 1925 it also began to invest in Canadian and American enterprises in order to maintain the supply of cargo.[46] The construction in 1921–22 of Manchester Liners House, next to the Royal Exchange, endowed the firm with a substantial real asset and a useful source of revenue, transforming it from tenant into landlord and returning 8 per cent gross on its investment through leases of the unoccupied portion.[47] The company also became the agents for a new Furness Withy service linking Vancouver to Manchester via the Panama Canal from 1924 as well as for a Houlder Bros. service linking Manchester to the river Plate from 1927 and paving the way for a joint venture into the chilled meat trade with the British & Argentine Steam Navigation Co. Ltd, which lasted for ten years from 1928.[48]

The large reserves of the company enabled it to survive the post-war depression in shipping and to maintain the payment of a regular

[43] M.L.B., 246–7, 6 September 1919. *The Times*, 26 June 1944, 6v. *The Complete Peerage* (London, St. Catherine Press, 1940), XIII, 510, 'Essendon'.

[44] M.L.B., 267–8, 9 March 1920; 271–2, 19 April 1920.

[45] Ibid., 289, 1 December 1920; 400, 13 April 1927.

[46] Ibid., 370, 28 September 1925; 375–6, 10 December 1925; 11, 19 September 1929; 25–26, 26 June 1930.

[47] Ibid., 309, 14 December 1921; 329, 27 June 1923.

[48] Ibid., 411–12, 6 January 1928; 120, 12 January 1938.

10 per cent dividend from 1923 to 1931 when most other companies were reducing or eliminating their dividends. Its contribution to the import tonnage of its home port declined, however, from 8.5 per cent in 1912–13 to 6 per cent in 1929 and it experienced keener competition from Liverpool. Its heavy dependence upon the Canadian grain trade presented a serious threat to its prosperity during the 1930s, when the high-cost arable farming of the prairies sank into its deepest depression and small foreign-flag vessels began, after the construction of the Welland Ship Canal (1914–32), to tap the cargo of the Canadian Lake ports before it reached Montreal.[49] The association with Furness Withy was maintained for forty years from 1919 through the sharing of a common chairman,[50] linking the fortunes of Manchester Liners with those of the largest British ship owners in the 1930s and reinforcing its security in a highly competitive business.

The war of 1939–45 cost the line half its fleet of ten vessels and enabled it to build up a large liquid reserve which was reconverted in the 1950s into fixed assets in the form of new vessels. The company began new services to the Canadian ports of the Great Lakes, especially Toronto, from 1952 and to the U.S. Lakes ports, especially Chicago, from 1956. In 1959 it supplied the first British vessel to traverse the new St Lawrence Seaway to Toronto. Manchester Liners remained relatively small in size but preserved the advantages of a very strong *esprit de corps*, reinforced by the institution of working directors from 1945 and by the creative leadership provided by the son and grandson of R. B. Stoker. Kenneth Stoker (1886–1979) served as managing director from 1932 until 1965 and also as a director of the Ship Canal Company (1936–70). Robert Burdon Stoker succeeded him in 1965, served as chairman from 1968 to 1979 and also officiated as president of the Manchester Chamber of Commerce in 1966–67, in the tradition of his grandfather. He boldly launched the company upon a new phase of dynamic expansion, based upon a

[49] Manchester Liners Ltd, *Shareholders' Minute Book*, 77–8, 2 October 1934.

[50] *The Times*, 30 March 1974, 16vii–viii, for the obituary of Sir Ernest H. Murrant (1889–1974), who succeeded Lord Essendon as chairman from 1944 to 1959.

pioneer deep-sea container service to Chicago in 1966 and to Montreal in 1969 and leading to the establishment in 1969 of a subsidiary, Manchester Liners (Canada) Ltd. Furness Withy supported that development by acquiring in 1968 Morrell Mills & Co. Ltd for the repair of both ships and containers, the Prince Line with its service to the Mediterranean and the agents of that line in Gough & Crosthwaite Ltd. The Manchester Prince Line was established and developed a thriving container trade to the Levant during the Middle East oil boom of the 1970s, tilting the balance of Manchester Liners' activity away from Canada towards Asia.[51] Furness Withy strengthened its links with the port of Manchester by converting Manchester Liners in 1970 from an associate into a subsidiary company, by dividing up the English market with the Canadian Pacific Railway from 1973 and by acquiring Manchester Dry Docks Ltd in 1974.

The enterprise of a relatively small firm of cargo liners in carrying the name of Manchester around the harbours of the world and in developing Anglo-Canadian trade has secured no recognition in the standard textbooks of English and Canadian economic history. Manchester Liners secured, however, its own reward for success: it survived in a hostile economic environment, carved out a secure niche for itself and attracted investment from Canada in 1974. Its ordinary dividends averaged 12 per cent per annum (1899–1977) and made it the most financially successful of the triad of firms associated with the Ship Canal.[52]

[51] R. B. Stoker, 'Changing Pattern of World Trade', *Transactions of the Manchester Statistical Society*, 11 November 1970, 1–20.

[52] Daniel Adamson left an estate of £54,169 in 1890, J. K. Bythell one of £18,563 in 1916 and Marshall Stevens one of £36,357 in 1936 but R. B. Stoker left one of £235,054 in 1919, having earned in addition to his salary a share in profits equivalent to a 2½ per cent ordinary dividend.

3

The growth of the import trade

The creation of a thriving inland port required not only the excavation of a seaway but also the construction of a complex of facilities and their integration into an existing structure of transport, commerce and industry. The commerce of the new port determined the nature of the terminal facilities required. That trade was essentially a transit trade and could best be accommodated in transit warehouses, so as to make the most effective use of the limited amount of land available at the docks, speed the turnover of goods and avoid any costly congestion. There was no prospect of any regular passenger traffic, as the short-lived Ship Canal Passenger Steamer Co. Ltd (1893–96) discovered.[1] The Canal had to attract and retain both an import and an export traffic and had in particular to equip itself to handle imports. Such facilities would include general warehouses for raw cotton and specialised facilities essential for the development of certain key trades such as grain elevators for the trade in wheat from America and India, cattle lairages, an abbattoir and oil storage tanks for the import of cattle and oil from North America, cold storage works for the preservation of frozen produce from Australasia and seed-crushing mills for the trade in oilseeds from India. The lairages were important for the development of trade not only with America but also with the Mediterranean because they would make possible a flow of American apples to complement the supply of Spanish oranges in order to create a flourishing fruit market in Manchester.

[1] T.L.P.C., 265–7, 24 April 1893; 64–5, 11 August 1893. B.O.D., 242, 18 January 1895; 250, 1 February; 429, 25 October. *Manchester Faces and Places*, vol. 5: 10, July 1894, 158–9, 'Manchester Ship Canal – The Passenger Traffic'.

The Canal Company had been unable to set aside enough funds to provide such facilities before the inauguration of the waterway but then found that it could not attract traffic until the facilities were available. The board of directors had resolved not to involve themselves in the promotion of warehouse or lighterage companies[2] but then discovered that outside capital would not finance the construction of any such buildings until the Canal had begun operations,[3] although the Canal could not extend its operations without the necessary equipment. The Company did provide tipping machinery at Partington for the export of coal but it had concluded contracts in 1893 for the building of only two sheds at the Manchester docks.[4] For imports Bythell at first preferred open-air storage to warehouses and then favoured the economical provision of a simple overhead covering rather than the building of a few fully equipped sheds with sides and paved flooring.[5] He was, however, forced to modify his sensible view by the determination of the Canal's clients to use its facilities as additional warehouse accommodation.

For the provision of the urgently needed facilities the Company turned both to the Corporation and to private enterprise. Through the appropriate committees the Corporation constructed four essential ancillary establishments, a fruit sale-room in 1894, a cold air store in 1895, cattle lairages in 1896 and oil storage tanks in 1897. That investment of municipal capital proved of lasting benefit through the stimulus it imparted to the import of fruit and oil. For other facilities the Company relied upon the enterprise of three private companies. The Manchester Ship Canal Pontoons & Dry Docks Co. Ltd was registered on 14 October 1891 by George Renwick (1850–1931)[6] of Newcastle and raised almost all its capital of £120,000 on Tyneside. It opened its first graving dock in 1894[7] and so supplied the port with

2 B.O.D., 34, 25 March 1892.
3 Ibid., 221, 3 March 1893.
4 Ibid., 262, 28 April 1893.
5 Ibid., 425, 24 November 1893; 93, 8 June 1894.
6 *The Times*, 20 June 1931, 14iv. *Burke's Peerage* (London, 1970, 105th edn.), 2246–7.
7 *Manchester City News*, 17 February 1894, 5vii.

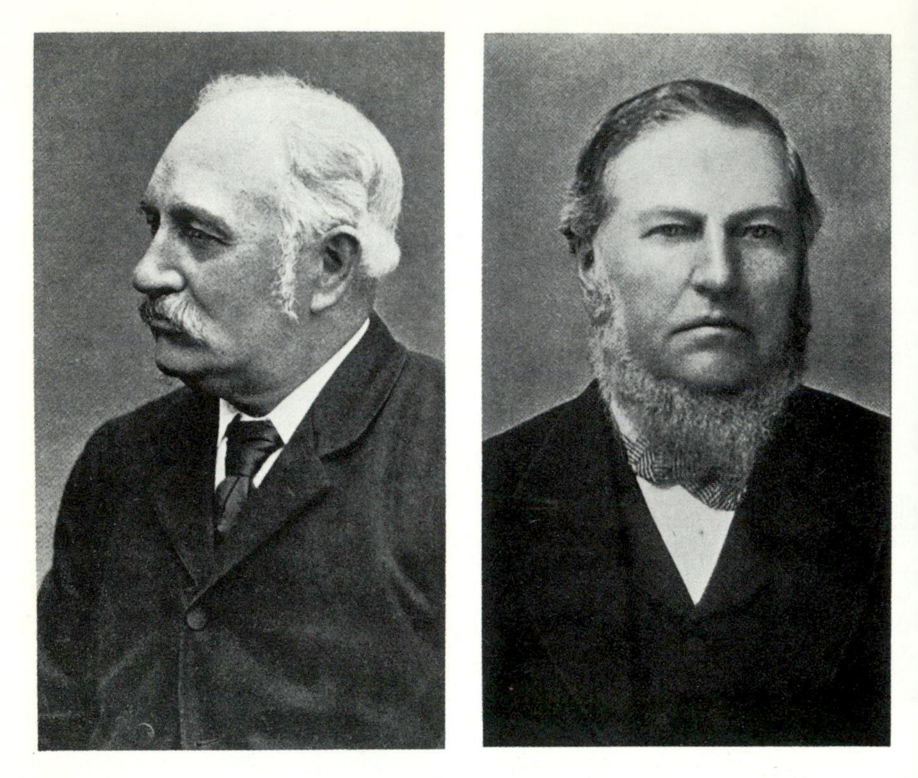

The founders of the Port of Manchester (*Leech, op. cit., i. 146; ii, 84; Manchester Central Library, Local History Collection; Trafford Park Estates Ltd*). From left to right:

Sir Edward Leader Williams, Chief Engineer, one of the five knights created in 1894 in recognition of services rendered in the completion of the Canal, the other four being Sir Anthony Marshall, Lord Mayor of Manchester, Sir William Bailey, Mayor of Salford, Sir Bosdin Leech and Sir Joseph Leigh, the son-in-law of Daniel Adamson.

Alderman Sir John J. Harwood, 'the Chamberlain of Manchester' (*Westminster Gazette*, 11 January 1894, iiii, 'Municipalities at Work. Manchester – I') who thrice served as mayor, in 1884–85, in 1887 and in 1887–88, being knighted in 1888. He was one of the first Corporation directors of the Canal Company appointed in 1891 and secured the creation on 11 December 1891 of a new Executive Committee, which was 'practically a Corporation Committee' (Leech, op. cit., ii, 106). As the chairman of the Executive

Committee and as deputy chairman of the Canal Company in 1893–94 he became 'the life and soul of the enterprise' and carried it to completion through his driving energy and his vast experience in construction works. He announced to the City Council on 4 October 1893 that the Ship Canal would be opened on New Year's Day, 1894, and he fixed 8 December 1893 as the day on which he intended to navigate the Canal from one end to the other. He also served as the chairman of the Waterworks Committee, completing the great Thirlmere aqueduct in 1894, that *annus mirabilis* in the history of Manchester, and as chairman of the Special Committee on Trafford Park (1893–96).

Robert B. Stoker, Managing Director (1898–1919) and Chairman (1913–19) of Manchester Liners Ltd.

Marshall Stevens, Manager of the Manchester Ship Canal (1885–96) and Managing Director (1897–1929) and Chairman (1912–29) of Trafford Park Estates Ltd.

an essential service: it suffered, however, from the slow development of traffic and was forced to seek financial relief from the Canal Company, which postponed filling the two seats alloted to it in 1891 on the board of directors until 1897.[8] For the first five years the firm paid no dividend to its ordinary shareholders but it became from 1900 the most successful of the Canal's three ancillary companies. It changed its name in 1906 to the Manchester Dry Docks Co. Ltd, added two more graving docks in 1907 and 1917[9] and reached the peak of its prosperity during the Great War, returning an average annual dividend of 8.7 per cent (1892–1968).[10]

The Manchester Ship Canal Warehousing Co. Ltd enjoyed closer relations with the Canal Company, being registered on 4 April 1895 by some of its large shareholders. That company filled the gap left by the failure of unaided private enterprise[11] and built the warehouses which were essential to attract trade, both general cargo and bulk imports of grain, cotton and sugar. The Canal Company employed a financial expedient of brilliant simplicity, devised by Bythell and based on the leasing of land within the docks to a syndicate at a nominal rent for ninety-nine years. The syndicate erected thereon warehouses according to the plans of the Company and then sub-let them on a repairing lease to the Company at an annual rent. The Company retained the option of purchasing the warehouses at cost price plus 10 per cent at twelve months' notice.[12] Thus it could prevent the intrusion of any alien company within the docks and could extend their equipment without any further issue of debentures at the expense of the ordinary shareholders. The first set of fifteen modern buildings, divided between multi-storeyed storage

[8] B.O.D., 209, 17 February 1893; 221, 3 March 1893; 232, 17 March 1893; 347, 31 December 1897; 381, 25 March 1898; 387, 15 April 1898.

[9] *Manchester Guardian*, 22 February 1907, 4vii. *The Engineer*, 1 June 1917, 492–3, 496.

[10] Excluding the nine years from 1920–21 to 1928–29, for which no dividends were published in the *Stock Exchange Official Yearbook*.

[11] B.O.D., 232–3, 17 March 1893; 148, 14 September 1894.

[12] Ibid., 244–5, 18 January 1895; 250–1, 1 February; 262, 15 February; 287, 22 March; 302–3, 5 April; 306, 26 April; 383, 2 August; 416, 27 September 1895; 22–26, 17 January 1896; 63, 14 February; 100, 5 June 1896; 222, 12 March 1897.

warehouses and single-storeyed transit sheds, were fully occupied from the time of their opening in mid-1896 and proved immediately profitable as the dry docks did not. The Warehouse Company began to receive the high rent of 5½ per cent with effect from 1 June 1896 and began to pay regular dividends from 1900. Such accommodation proved more necessary in Manchester than in Liverpool because of the disposition of importers to remove their cargo only slowly from the docks. The Canal Company could not afford to levy a heavy charge for demurrage and thus became a captive of the merchants on whose custom it depended.

In 1897 the Warehouse Company agreed to erect additional warehouses at a cost of £150,000 but at a lower rental of 4 per cent, so raising its capital from £100,000 to £250,000. It was then persuaded to use £100,000 of the money to build an essential grain elevator.[13] As a business concern it proved less profitable than the dry docks company, paying an average annual dividend of 6 per cent for forty years until the blitz of 1940 destroyed the elevator. In effect it became a financial company and enjoyed an existence of fifty-four years, winding up in 1949 and transferring its remaining warehouses to the Canal Company. Its achievement had been to prove the practicability of the 'warehousing system' of a sub-lease and thus to encourage its extension to an even bolder venture. The Manchester Dock & Warehouse Extension Co. Ltd was registered by the same friends of the Canal on 29 July 1902 and shared the same secretary as the Warehouse Company in W. H. Shaw. Its capital was £250,000 and its function was to undertake the construction of No. 9 dock and its warehouses.[14] Thus it prevented the new dock from becoming a charge on revenue before its completion but helped to raise the rent paid by the Canal Company to 10 per cent of its expenditure in 1906.[15] It crowned its first achievement by the construction in 1912–15 of a second elevator at the head of the new dock. For the sixty-six years from 1902 it paid an average dividend of 4.6 per cent: then in

[13] Ibid., 228–9, 26 March 1897; 304–5, 17 September 1897.
[14] Ibid., 72–4, 30 May 1902.
[15] Ibid., 403–4, 8 February 1907; 4, 2 August 1907.

1968 it began a new career as the Bridgewater Investment Trust Ltd.

The completion of the port's basic terminal facilities in 1898 coincided with the inauguration of the underground branch line of the Lancashire & Yorkshire Railway from Windsor Bridge to Salford Docks[16] and with the establishment of Manchester Liners. Under such stimuli imports experienced a distinct boom and from 1899 expanded faster than exports, rising to form 62 per cent of the volume of the Canal's trade and 67 per cent of its value in 1900–03. In value imports increased even faster than in volume, expanding between 1894 and 1913 almost 60 per cent faster on average than exports. They proved easier to attract than exports because they were shipped in bulk. Manchester became more important as a port of import than as one of export: as a port of export it rose in status from the tenth largest in 1894 to the eighth in 1903, while as a port of import it soared during its first decade of operation from the seventeenth largest to the fourth in 1903, so establishing the position which it thereafter maintained. Imports increased in their relative importance for forty years, rising to form their peak proportion of 79 per cent of total traffic, by value in 1937 and by volume in 1941.

The import trade proved of great benefit, directly and indirectly, to the working classes and to their representative wholesale organisation. The C.W.S. remained a staunch supporter of the Canal and secured continuous representation upon the Canal Company's board of directors from 1893 until 1945. It used the waterway for imports rather than for exports. On 1 January 1894 it brought up from Rouen, the Cottonopolis of France, the *Pioneer*, which became the first merchant vessel registered in the new port, the first to reach it from overseas and the first to unload cargo, one of cube sugar.[17] The C.W.S. pioneered the industrial development of the banks of the Canal by its establishment in 1894 at Irlam of a soap works, which imported resin from 1895 and expanded into margarine manufacture

[16] *Manchester Guardian*, 29 March 1898, 9iv; 30 March, 7vii.

[17] P. Redfern, *The Story of the C.W.S. The Jubilee History of the Co-operative Wholesale Society Ltd, 1863–1913* (Manchester, C.W.S., 1913), 134–5, 166, 241, 307.

[18] B.O.D., 314–315, 26 April 1895; 135–6, 2 January 1914.

from 1914.[18] It also bought land in 1903 at Trafford Wharf, where it opened in 1906 both a flour mill and a bacon factory. The increase in imports extended employment rather than destroying it, supplying far more foodstuffs and raw materials than manufactures and creating a regional boom in the haulage industry. Thus the number of carriers and their agents in Manchester increased from 61 in 1894 to 94 in 1904 and to 151 in 1914. The associated development of the city's function as a distributive centre was facilitated by the organisation of produce exchanges and trade associations: it was actively encouraged by both the C.W.S. and the local banks.[19] That trend enhanced the commercial status of the city within the region at the expense of Liverpool and Preston, the older capitals of Lancashire: it compensated Cottonopolis for the relative decline of the home trade in textiles and of the trade in domestic grain, fostering in their stead the development of the functions of a regional metropolis.

The importance of the import trade may have been underestimated by the traditional emphasis upon the exporting function of Lancashire industry and by a comparative neglect of the massive consuming power developed amongst 'the first industrial society' in the history of the world. That vast army of consumers remained when 'the generals and rulers of human toil',[20] the Manchester merchants, had gone the way of the captains and the kings. Their voracious appetite, at home and at work, could be curbed only by the impact of world war and thus established the pre-eminence of imports in the traffic of the Canal.

The predominance of imports determined the rhythm of movement of the Canal's traffic, moulding both seasonal and cyclical fluctuations. The stabilising influence of general cargo, which gave variety to the trade of older ports, was absent for the first thirty years of the Canal's history. The activity of the port served as an economic barometer, registering the movement of the trade cycle as well as the impact of war. A study of the ten successive recessions recorded in Table 2 permits certain conclusions to be drawn. The distinctive

[19] *Manchester Guardian*, 5 February 1902, 10ii–iii, 'Manchester Banks and the Ship Canal. The Financing of Imports'.

[20] H. Taine, *Notes sur l'Angleterre* (Paris, Hachette, 1872), 295.

Table 2

Periodic recessions in the traffic of the Port of Manchester, 1901–61 (%)

Year	*Volume*	*Value*	*Share of imports in the loss of volume*	*Share of imports in the loss of value*
1901	3·6	3·4	93·6*	153
1908	12·4	14·5	87·6*	69·7
1914–18	39·5	+90·2	51·9*	84·5
1921	24·9	58·4	65·5	70·9
1927	6·6	2·1	231	222·9
1929–33	14·2	51·7	75·5*	58·3
1938	9·1	19·6	63·3	81·2
1940–46	30·2	+76·2	79·6	69·8*
1957	9·0	+9·8	50·6	254·8
1960–61	19·7	5·7	100·2	56

*Percentage contribution of exports and not of imports to the loss of traffic.
Source: Manchester Ship Canal Company, *Traffic Statistics, 1894–1964. Annual Statements of Trade*, 1900–1961.

impact of two world wars was drastically to reduce the volume of traffic but to raise its value in compensation. That phenomenon did not occur in peacetime until 1957 in the wake of the sharp rise in oil prices induced by the Suez crisis. Two of the ten depressions stand out as unexampled in their severity: that of 1921 slashed the value of trade by £121 million, while that of 1960–61 reduced the tonnage of cargo by 3.64 million tons. The dominant influence of imports is clearly apparent, since they receded in every depression and were responsible for the decline in the value of trade in seven out of eight cases, while exports twice rose in value, in 1901 and 1927, as the value of imports sank. Exports tended to follow the pattern of imports, except in 1927 and 1960–61, when exports rose in volume as imports shrank. A reduction in exports did, however, reduce the total volume of traffic during the first three depressions, in 1901, 1908 and 1914–

18, establishing a pattern repeated in the world depression of 1929–32. Those recessions were caused by the loss of coal shipments in 1901 and 1908 and by the loss of textile exports in 1929–33. The typical import-led depression appeared in 1921, 1927 and 1938 with the reduction in cotton and timber imports in 1921 and 1938 and with the disappearance of coal imports in 1927. The pre-war pattern reappeared in 1957 and 1960–61 with the reduction in oil imports. The fluctuations in the traffic of the port harmonised with those of national commerce from 1908 until 1946. The recession of 1901 was, however, peculiar to Manchester and that of 1927 was much more severe in Manchester than in the trade of the kingdom as a whole. Both those recessions were the product of a decline in coal shipments, that of 1901 in coal exports and that of 1927 in coal imports.

For the first thirty years of the Canal's history imports were dominated by a seasonal influx of timber, grain and raw cotton. Timber had been expected to supply the Canal with a large traffic, and imports fulfilled those expectations, providing the largest single tonnage from 1894 until 1910 and ranking second from 1910 until

Table 3

Share of the main imports in the total import trade of the Canal, 1895–1913

Commodity	*Volume* (%)	*Value* (%)
Timber	16·68	5·05
Grain	14·86	10·10
Cotton	6·92	40·53
Oil	6·6	3·4
Total	38,896,883 tons	£398,243,015

Source: Manchester Ship Canal, *Traffic Statistics, 1894–1913*. *Annual Statements of Trade*, 1895–1913.

Cargo tonnage of the Port of Manchester, 1894–1977.

1924. Wood supplied an ideal cargo because it was heavy and bulky in proportion to its value and therefore employed much more shipping tonnage than cotton. It required no elaborate wharfside installations, since storage in the open air proved beneficial rather than harmful to softwood by allowing it to season. The Canal Company encouraged the trade by the grant of free wharfage for the first fifteen months of operation in return for a relatively high toll. Alderman J. W. Southern, timber merchant and deputy chairman of the Canal Company, fostered the development of the trade and pioneered from 1897 the use of Trafford Park by timber firms.[21] The trade established itself on a firm basis during the very first summer of the Canal's existence, supplying a large, diverse and expanding demand in the Manchester district. That demand was for an instrumental commodity essential to the trade of East Lancashire, which formed 'one huge industrial town' and was 'assuredly the greatest wood-consuming district in the world'.[22] Timber was used in the coopering trade serving the breweries, in the manufacture of packing-cases for textile shipments, in engineering and, above all, in the building industry.

Manchester entered into competition with Hull as well as with Liverpool in its efforts to secure a trade which had hitherto flowed from the Baltic into the ports of the east coast and from North America into the ports of the west coast. Despite the initial opposition of Liverpool shipbrokers to Manchester charters,[23] imports developed because the trade remained more dependent than any other upon cheap carriage. They were carried first by 'tramps' rather than by 'liners' and were borne by sail to Runcorn, for lightering up to Manchester: they came first from the Baltic during 1894 and then from North America during 1895, when Liverpool's imports of timber sank as those of Manchester rose from one-seventh to form nearly a quarter of those of Liverpool. Manchester rose in status from the twentieth largest timber port in 1894 to the ninth in 1895, the eighth in 1896, the seventh in 1898 and, during the six years of continuing expansion from 1901, to the fourth in 1904. Increasingly its imports of timber were brought by steamer, especially from the Baltic, direct to Manchester, so saving the cost of lighterage and increasing the revenues of the Canal Company.[24] The trade never,

[21] B.O.D., 158, 28 September 1894. *Northern Finance and Trade*, 22 December 1897, 521.

[22] 'Lumber' [H. H. Sales], *Manchester a Timber Port* (London, Rider, 1884, 15 pp.), 11.

[23] T.R.C., 156, 5 April 1894.

[24] B.O.D., 412, 27 September 1895.

however, reached more than half the volume anticipated by Marshall Stevens in 1891 and suffered from certain intrinsic shortcomings. It had established itself so securely during 1894 that it expanded thereafter more slowly than any other main import and achieved its greatest relative importance during 1897 after four years of continuous expansion. Timber and pulp supplied 33 per cent of the increment in import tonnage between 1894 and 1897 and 30 per cent of the import tonnage in 1897.

The trade remained essentially seasonal because both the Baltic and the St Lawrence froze over during the winter. Timber thus supplied the bulk of cargo carried along the Canal during the summer, when traffic reached the peak level of its activity before receding in September. The importers of timber were divided between small and large merchants. The small customers represented the local timber trade, which was almost as democratic in recruitment as the building trade: they handled the typical Manchester trade, importing small parcels and dealing in inferior timber, especially for case-making. Large importers were attracted to the port of Manchester from Liverpool by its facilities for the ready handling of stock and for ex-ship delivery direct to orders or to the yards and by reductions in charges offered upon large-scale imports. Timber imports made full use of the port's facilities, when other trades remained undeveloped, by employing the wharves rather than public or private yards for purposes of storage. The charging of quay rent by the Canal Company led to the formation in March 1895 of the first Manchester Timber Trade Association under the auspices of Alderman Southern but produced little more economical use of quay space. A severe blockage at the docks created by large imports from America in 1899 encouraged Bythell and Southern to provide six timber pontoons as floating wharves and to project the construction of the new No. 9 dock as a timber dock, with additional open storage space to the north on the site of the future dock No. 10 for the needs of the trade.

Unlike the other bulk import trades in grain and oil, timber shipments remained heavily dependent upon dock labour. The highly skilled 'lumpers' employed in the demanding task of unloading secured increased rates of pay after strikes in 1896 and 1907 but not after one in 1913.[25] Imports were dominated until the 1920s by the cheaper woods, while Liverpool remained predominantly an importer of the finer and more valuable hardwood. Manchester did not replace Garston as a timber entrepôt for the Midlands and did not make its docks into 'the timber depot for the Midland and Northern counties'.[26] Imports proved sensitive to the competition of other ports and remained liable to marked fluctuations in annual volume, varying between 1898 and 1914 in inverse ratio to the imports of grain. Thus a decline in timber and pulp imports by 5 per cent in 1898 was offset only by increased imports of cotton, grain and oil: another decline, by 15 per cent in 1901, was not fully counterbalanced by an increase in the import of cement and stone setts, so causing the first recession in the import tonnage of the Canal. Another decline in timber and pulp imports, by 11 per cent in 1909, was, however, largely offset by an increase in imports of cotton and grain.

Timber imports remained low in value, ranking in total value after raw cotton from 1894, after grain from 1898 and after oil from 1921. The trade extended its market to the Midlands with the advent of the motor lorry and the increase in overside delivery ex-ship. It remained buoyant until 1928 and reached successively higher peaks in 1913, 1923 and 1937. The imports of 1927 supplied the Canal Company with 8.25 per cent of its net revenue from 7 per cent of its total tonnage. Even during 1927 imports of timber increased much more to Liverpool, Garston and Preston than to Manchester because the large importers were attracted by lower port charges.[27] Those importers continued to favour the competitors of Manchester, especially Garston, so that timber imports into Manchester declined by 39.4 per cent between 1928 and 1931 while timber sank in status from the third largest import to the sixth. The Canal Company abolished the penalty rents it had instituted in 1916[28] but did not

[25] Ibid., 112–13, 10 July 1896; 470–2, 12 July 1907; 49–50, 5 September 1913; 76–7, 26 September.

[26] *Manchester City News*, 22 September 1894, 5i.

[27] Manchester Timber Trade Association, *Minutes*, vol. 5, 62, 19 April 1928; 159, 12 December 1929.

[28] Ibid., vol. 5, 167, 16 January 1930.

reduce its other charges sufficiently to satisfy the second Manchester Timber Trade Association, which had been founded in 1917.[29] The local timber trade had enjoyed very close relations with the Canal Company in contrast to the lack of co-operation between the Liverpool Timber Trade Association, formed in 1877, and the Mersey Docks & Harbour Board.[30] During the depression of 1931 the Manchester Association established a special Ship Canal Comittee[31] which held eighteen conferences with the officials of the Canal Company during 1932[32] and succeeded in securing a reduction in storage charges which were of particular importance to those importers without any yards of their own. The new schedule of charges, coupled with the stimulus of imperial preference and a boom in building fostered by Manchester's suburban expansion and Simon's Wythenshawe housing scheme, produced six years of increasing imports, doubling their tonnage between 1931 and 1937 and raising them in 1937 to an all-time peak of 521,000 tons or 10 per cent of total imports. The import of hardwood began to increase after the establishment of furniture manufacture in Trafford Park in 1929 and the expansion of woodworking industries. The Canal Company became, however, inclined to cultivate more profitable traffic such as that in oil, cotton and provisions.[33] It had only a limited area of land available for use as public yards and sought to encourage delivery ex-quay or ex-steamer. Its insistence that the quays should be cleared as soon as possible and should not be used as a sorting ground encouraged importers to acquire or extend their own private yards. It could not compete with Garston in its low charges for ex-ship deliveries to large importers.[34]

Imports of timber declined from their peak level of 1937 after the Canal Company raised its charges[35] and were surpassed in tonnage by sand and gravel from 1939 as cement became an increasingly

[29] Ibid., vol. 1, 74–5, 1 March 1918.
[30] Ibid., vol. 8, 5 December 1960.
[31] Ibid., vol. 6, 83, 1 October 1931.
[32] Ibid., vol. 6, 158a–d, 12 May 1932 – 250–2, 8 December 1932.
[33] Ibid., vol. 6, 388, 19 April 1934; 400–06, 9 May 1934.
[34] Ibid., vol. 6, 628–30, 25 June 1936; 658–63, 12 October 1936.
[35] Ibid., vol. 6, 754, 23 September 1937; 764, 21 October 1937.

popular substitute for wood in building. Then the war of 1939–45 weakened the connection between the timber trade and the port. Home-grown timber became the main source of supply to the trade, while Canada became the main source of timber imports. The dispersal of stocks from the port area as a precaution against incendiary attack from the air[36] permanently reduced the accommodation available to the trade. Imports declined from their post-war peak of 1947 after the Company raised charges by 41 per cent in order to eliminate the heavy losses incurred in the labour-intensive handling of timber.[37] The advent of the bulk carriage of timber from British Columbia to Liverpool in 1967 reduced imports to Manchester even further. The Manchester Timber Trade Association undertook negotiations for a merger with the Liverpool Timber Trade Association in order to form the North West Timber Trade Association and to show by the change in its name from 1971 that it was not concerned solely with the Port of Manchester.[38] The Canal Company had been forced to sacrifice an old-established but labour-intensive and unprofitable trade in order to maintain its operations on an economic basis.

The trade had, however, established an important and enduring connection between Manchester and the Baltic. It also enabled the port to develop a traffic in the by-products of timber, in paper and in paper-making materials, especially pulp. The trade in wood-pulp from Norway was secured only after great effort in competition with Fleetwood as well as with Liverpool and Hull by arranging through railway and canal rates to Leeds.[39] That success by Manchester provoked an immediate response from Thomas Wilson & Sons of Hull, which decided to run three competing lines from Manchester to the ports of Russia, Sweden and Norway.[40] Pulp imports developed to such an extent that Manchester seemed likely in 1897 to become the

[36] Ibid., vol. 7, 1086–9, 16 September 1940.

[37] Ibid., vol. 7, 1408–10, 20 January 1948.

[38] Ibid., vol. 9, 25 February 1970.

[39] B.O.D., 163, 166, 19 October 1894; 257, 15 February 1895; 284, 22 March 1895; 468, 22 November 1895. *Manchester Guardian*, 5 September 1895, 6iv, 'Effect of the Canal on the Trade of Hull'.

[40] B.O.D., 283, 22 March 1895; 334–5, 24 May; 9, 20 December 1895.

leading pulp port of the kingdom.[41] Those imports reached an early peak in 1900 which was surpassed only in 1932. They fluctuated in harmony with the imports of timber, unlike the imports of other paper-making materials. They never outweighed the volume of paper because Lancashire papermakers remained firmly settled in the old commercial grooves.[42] Wood-pulp and other paper-making materials nevertheless supplied, together with timber, 25 per cent of the Canal's tonnage of imports during its first twenty years from 1894 to 1913. The import of paper began from Finland in July 1894[43] and supplied a steady demand in the Manchester area. Pulp imports began to expand markedly with the establishment of Bowater's paper mill at Ellesmere Port in 1931 and of Courtauld's rayon works at Preston in 1935. They even surpassed the tonnage of timber imports from 1949, rising from the eighth largest import in 1948 to the fourth in 1960 and becoming the residual heir of the port's original staple traffic.

Imports of grain were secured only in the course of a long struggle against the competition of Liverpool. They increased in volume to supply the port with its third largest import from 1896 and its second largest from 1898. Only in 1910 did they become the leading import in succession to timber and establish the dominant position they retained until 1925. The battle to secure those imports was waged against the vested interests of the milling industry in the seaboard ports which had been created as a direct result of the successful campaign waged by the Manchester-based Anti-Corn Law League for the repeal of the Corn Laws. Liverpool in particular had established in the 1860s a large milling industry for the supply of flour to its hinterland and had become since 1873 the main port for the import of grain. Thus grain, unlike cotton or timber, had never provided the Bridgewater Canal with a large traffic. The new port of Manchester could acquire a trade in foreign grain only by providing superior

[41] E. Deiss, *À Travers l'Angleterre Industrielle et Commerciale* (*Notes de Voyage*) (Paris, Guillaumin, 1898), 202 note.

[42] B.O.D., 468, 22 November 1895.

[43] Ibid., 166, 19 October 1894.

facilities to those of Liverpool. The town had, however, no large grain merchants able to buy full cargoes of grain abroad and to distribute them piecemeal to millers. Nor could the small buyers of the district be persuaded to combine for the purpose of joint import and so to moderate their competitive individualism. Above all, there were no storage facilities for grain at the docks, and several successive attempts during the first four years of the Canal's operation to form companies for the construction of grain silos failed.[44] The grain trade could develop upon any scale only after the construction first of an elevator and then of flour mills. Imports enjoyed six years of uninterrupted expansion from 1894 to 1900 but largely comprised feed grain for livestock while Liverpool retained the much more valuable trade in food grains for human consumption. The Mersey Docks & Harbour Board responded to the arrival in May 1895 of the first bulk shipment of Californian wheat, brought by sail to Runcorn for barging up to Manchester, by deciding on 13 June to reduce its charges on wheat by 25 per cent.[45]

The first real stimulus to the grain trade was given by the increase in the imports of raw cotton during 1896. The vessels carrying cotton required ballast, which could most usefully be supplied by grain. The large imports of both cotton and grain during the last quarter of 1896 created a terrible blockage at the docks because of the sheer lack of accommodation. The construction of an elevator became an urgent necessity but would require a large investment of capital which the Canal Company itself could not afford. At that critical juncture Salford Corporation decided on 14 October 1896 to finance the building of such a silo but was forced on 17 May 1897 by opposition from local Socialists to abandon the scheme.[46] Bythell promptly held two emergency meetings of the board of directors on 3 and 4 June in order to take the necessary steps to preserve the grain trade of the port. The Warehouse Company was persuaded to use the funds earmarked

[44] T.R.C., 35, 5 July 1894; B.O.D., 177, 19 October 1894; 300, 5 April 1895; 306, 26 April 1895.

[45] B.O.D., 311, 26 April 1895; 330–1, 24 May; 349, 21 June 1895.

[46] Ibid., 148, 23 October 1896; 156, 6 November; 173–4, 10 December 1896; 205–6, 12 February 1897; 251, 21 May; 263, 4 June 1897.

for the erection of additional warehouse accommodation for the construction of a silo.[47] The largest elevator in Europe was designed by John S. Metcalf (1847–1912) of Chicago, 'who was believed to be the cleverest elevator engineer in America',[48] but took twice as long to complete as had been estimated because its foundations had to be sunk very much deeper than expected in treacherous ground. An immense ten-storeyed timber tower, with sloping shoulders and a marine leg for automatic unloading, planted upon Trafford Wharf an example of the most typical architecture of the Canadian prairies.[49]

The new building was first used on the anniversary of American independence, 4 July 1898,[50] and was soon in full employment, releasing space in the sheds for other cargo and earning the expected rent for its proprietor from the Canal Company. It proved a great success, especially in speeding discharge and delivery, but entailed a heavy cost in fire insurance on what remained until its destruction by enemy action in 1940 'a splendid fire pile'[51] because the grain merchants had objected to the use of concrete bins, insisting upon wooden ones. Grain imports doubled in volume between 1897 and 1903, ranking from 1898 second to timber in tonnage and second to cotton in value. Wheat imports, carried by the new Canadian service of Manchester Liners, surpassed maize imports from 1899 until 1960 and began from 1903 to attract the milling industry towards the docks and especially to the vicinity of the elevator. In turn the development of the milling industry made possible the export of flour and meal from Manchester, first recorded in 1904, and stimulated the development in Trafford Park of such subsidiary industries as the manufacture of biscuits from 1905 and of corn products from 1911. The industry found, however, its primary market in the flour dealers and bakers and ultimately in the immense demand for bread of the largest urban industrial population of the kingdom.

[47] Ibid., 256–7, 3 June 1897; 259–61, 4 June; 276–81, 2 July; 286–7, 16 July 1897.

[48] Ibid., 261, 4 June 1897, J. K. Bythell.

[49] *Manchester Evening Mail*, 15 February 1898, 6ii–iii. *Manchester Guardian*, 1 July 1898, 7vi. *The Engineer*, 7 October 1898, 354–6.

[50] *Manchester Guardian*, 8 July 1898, 5iv. B.O.D., 413, 15 July 1898.

[51] *Manchester Evening Mail*, 15 February 1898, 6iii.

The trade remained dependent upon imports of cotton because full cargoes of grain from American ports could not be secured. Liverpool successfully preserved its vast grain trade by quoting the lowest possible freights for grain from New York and by reducing all its charges. Thus it captured most of the new trade in wheat and maize from the Argentine and expanded the milling industry of Birkenhead on a large scale, remaining the premier grain port of the kingdom until

The terminal docks, 1929 (*Manchester Ship Canal Company*). The aerial view shows to the left Salford Quay (1,100 ft), No. 9 dock (1905, 2,700 ft × 250 ft) and the site for No. 10 dock in use as a timber storage ground. An early use of reinforced concrete on the Hennebique system was made in the construction of the transit warehouses (1902–04) to the south of No. 9 dock and of No. 2 grain elevator (1912–15) at its head. Above Mode Wheel Locks lie the three dry docks (1894, 1907, 1917), with the floating pontoon dock (1894) of Manchester Dry Docks Co. Ltd (1891–1979). South of the graving docks lies the Foreign Animals Wharf (1896), while to the north is No. 1 grain elevator (1898), with the Hovis flour mill (1906) to the rear and the marshalling yards of Trafford Park below.

1921.[52] The boom in grain imports to Manchester in 1902–03 brought the first shipments of Indian grain up the Canal and encouraged the Canal Company to lay the foundations of a second elevator at the end of the new No. 9 dock, facing the first elevator on Trafford Wharf and supplying Salford Docks with what its Corporation had renounced in 1897. Then a sharp recession in imports in 1904–05 compelled the Company to defer construction.[53] From 1908, however, imports expanded for seven successive years, stimulated by a large extension of the local milling industry and by the rise of Canada in 1912–19 to the position of the second source of supply of wheat to the British market. The opening in 1906 of the Hovis mill on Trafford Wharf, linked by underground conveyor belt to the elevator just to the north, created the nucleus of the Rank-Hovis-McDougall complex and was followed by the establishment of four more mills in 1911–13. The purchase of the Sun Mill by the C.W.S. in 1906 established co-operative milling in Manchester and ended inland milling at Rochdale and Oldham: the doubling of the Sun Mill in 1913 made it the largest mill in the kingdom, with its own wharf, elevator and silos.[54] The construction of the second elevator in reinforced concrete was authorised on 15 March 1912 and undertaken on behalf of the Manchester Dock & Warehouse Extension Co. Ltd by Henry Simon Ltd, which had failed to secure the contract for the building of the first elevator.[55] The best equipped elevator in the world came into use from September 1915,[56] discharging grain twice as fast as its precursor. The record imports of grain during 1916 were surpassed only in 1924, but grain retained the dominance it had established over timber. The Canal secured a fair share of the trade in grain and the Canal Company derived from it more revenue than from timber. For thirty-two years from 1898 to 1929 grain supplied

[52] G. C. Allen, (ed.), *The Import Trade of the Port of Liverpool. Future Prospects* (University Press of Liverpool, 1946), 66.

[53] B.O.D., 325–7, 9 October 1903; 332–3, 23 October 1903; 420–2, 25 March 1904; 207, 3 November 1905; 380, 7 December 1906.

[54] P. Redfern, *The Story of the C.W.S.* (1913), 224–5, 237–8.

[55] B.O.D., 245–51, 15 March 1912; 272, 26 April; 354–65, 25 October 1912.

[56] Ibid., 187–9, 23 March 1914; 415–17, 2 July 1915; 442–3, 27 August; 452, 24 September 1915.

the port with its second most valuable import to cotton: for fifteen years from 1910 to 1924 it remained the main import of the port, supplying during those years 18.7 per cent of the total tonnage of imports as well as 6.4 per cent of the gross imports of grain into Great Britain.

The trade remained much more buoyant than the timber trade: it survived the decline of the cotton trade and expanded as Canada established its primacy in the import trade in 1930. It benefited by the extension in 1931 of the Liverpool grain futures contract to include Manchester and by the grant of a preference on imperial wheat (1932–38), benefiting not only Canada at the expense of the U.S.A. and the Argentine but also the winter ports of St John and Halifax at the expense of U.S. ports. Imports enjoyed five successive years of expansion from 1932 to reach a peak in 1936 as Canada became the supplier to a world ravaged by crop failure. The establishment of Kellogg's new factory on the Barton Dock Estate in 1937–38 for the supply of the European market increased the import of maize and contributed to the post-war expansion of imports from 1953 to an all-time peak level during 1970, forty years after the national peak level of imports in 1931. Manchester then ranked as the sixth grain port of the kingdom and had achieved greater relative importance in the grain trade than in the timber trade.

In the direct import of other foodstuffs Manchester accomplished less than it achieved in the grain trade but it proved more successful in the import of fruit, provisions and tea than in that of meat or sugar. The import of foreign cattle was the only trade requiring the explicit permission of the State under the Contagious Diseases (Animals) Act of 1878: it was, however, vital to the American trade because freights ruled so low in the most competitive market in the shipping world that voyage-profits could only be gleaned by the carriage of cattle. The establishment of a Foreign Animals Wharf was sanctioned by the Board of Agriculture on 20 December 1893 but the construction of the necessary lairages, just west of the dry dock at Mode Wheel Locks, required twenty-five months because of difficulties in drainage.[57] The first cattle steamers did not arrive from New York until eight months after the opening of the lairages on 26 August 1896[58] and the trade was developed only by Manchester Liners from 1898 and by Lamport & Holt from 1903. The import of cattle had risen to a national peak in 1890 and reached its maximum level into Manchester in 1905 when measured by value and in 1908 according to the number of oxen. Liverpool had, however, retained the vast bulk of the cattle trade, investing lavishly in new lairages at Seacombe[59] and capturing the new trade in chilled and frozen meat. The import of livestock to Manchester ended when the Board of Agriculture prohibited the trade after the introduction of foot-and-mouth disease in live cattle from Ireland.[60]

The import of frozen meat promised to be the most remunerative of all trades to the Canal Company and was repeatedly pursued but to little avail. That traffic required the establishment of a shipping line from either Australia or the Argentine, the provision of cold storage and the supply of specialised marketing facilities. The Corporation of Manchester pushed ahead the construction of Cold Storage Buildings and inaugurated them on 23 April 1895.[61] But the associated Australia–Manchester steamship service was not established by the Federal-Houlder-Shire Line until 1904 and even then the Ship Canal failed to become the expected 'highway for argosies laden with the refrigerated produce of New Zealand and Australia'.[62] The cold stores erected at Mode Wheel in 1897–98 by the Colonial Consignment & Distributing Co. Ltd[63] were taken over by the Union Cold Storage Co. Ltd, the powerful Vesty trust, and were practically never

57 Ibid., 64, 20 May 1892; 283, 22 March 1895; 373, 19 July; 436, 25 October 1895; 26, 17 January 1896; 53, 31 January 1896.

58 *Manchester City News*, 29 August 1896, 6vii. *Manchester Guardian*, 27 April 1897, 9vii.

59 B.O.D., 192, 16 November 1894.

60 Ibid., 315, 5 July 1912; 345–6, 27 September 1912; 393–4, 6 December 1912.

61 *Manchester Guardian*, 24 April 1895, 6ii–iii.

62 J. T. Critchell and J. Raymond, *A History of the Frozen Meat Trade* (London, Constable, 1912; Dawson, 1969), 223, 418.

63 *Manchester Guardian*, 14 November 1898, 6vi.

used after the end of the Plate venture (1904–08) of Manchester Liners. Nor did the sorting chamber for frozen produce established by the Canal Company in a transit shed in 1906 succeed in undermining Liverpool's hold upon the import of frozen meat.[64] Lard was, however, imported from Chicago in 1894 for Kilvert's, who established a factory in Trafford Park in 1899 and helped to increase the import of lard until it ranked second in value only to grain amongst foodstuffs.

The fruit trade of Manchester was created by the Canal and proved as profitable as the import of raw cotton but remained as seasonal a traffic as the import of frozen meat. It began with the import of currants from Patras on 5 October 1894 for the C.W.S. to meet the demand for the Christmas season and with the import of oranges from Spain after the opening on 8 November of the Corporation's Fruit Sale-room at Campfield.[65] The trade in green fruit far surpassed in volume that in dried fruit but required the winter shipment of apples from America to complement the import of oranges from Valencia. The import of apples in turn was dependent upon the establishment of the cattle trade from America and remained a near-monopoly of Liverpool and London. The import of bananas from Jamaica began first to Bristol in 1901 and was extended to Manchester in 1902 by Elders & Fyffes (Shipping) Ltd, in association with the United Fruit Company, the greatest trust of the Caribbean world.[66] That trade made Manchester the leading banana port of the kingdom in 1906 and raised the total volume of fruit imports to a peak in 1911, when the port lost that lucrative traffic to Garston, with its faster and cheaper facilities for shipment by rail.[67]

The supply of provisions to the British market was divided

[64] B.O.D., 283–4, 6 April 1904. Manchester Association of Importers and Exporters, *Minutes*, 15 January 1914, Minute No. 77.

[65] *Manchester Guardian*, 5 October 1894, 7vii; 9 November, 7i–ii. B.O.D., 190, 16 November 1894. P. Redfern, *The Story of the C.W.S.* (1913), 166.

[66] B.O.D., 67, 9 May 1902; 473, 29 July 1904; 477, 2 September 1904; 124, 5 May 1905. T. M. Young, *Manchester and the Atlantic Traffic* (Manchester, Sherratt, 1902), 75–84.

[67] B.O.D., 419–20, 22 July 1910; 451–2, 14 October 1910; 61–2, 28 April 1911.

between Denmark and Ireland. Manchester was able to secure a foothold in that remunerative traffic only by importing provisions from America. Butter was not imported from New Zealand until 1923, nor from Australia until 1934, because there were no large importers of foodstuffs in the Manchester area apart from the C.W.S. Beet sugar formed one of the first cargoes carried up the Canal on the day of its inauguration and supplied a vast local demand, increasing the volume of direct imports to a peak in 1914. Manchester could, however, import only refined sugar and could not compete with the traditional staple of Liverpool's West India trade. After 1914 Liverpool increased its share of sugar imports at the expense of Manchester,[68] whose imports declined rapidly after 1925 and were surpassed from 1927 by those of tea. Imports of tea had long been sought by the Canal Company but were not secured until 1918, when imports reached an all-time peak, being maintained thereafter by the enterprise of Brooke Bond in Trafford Park and of the C.W.S. in Ordsall.[69] Another beverage was stout, which was imported from Guinness's brewery in Dublin from 1904. A steep rise in freights inspired Guinness to lease nearly one-tenth of Trafford Park in 1913 and to project the erection of a huge brewery, served by its own wharf on the Ship Canal. The frustration of that plan by the outbreak of war enabled imports of stout to continue, reaching their all-time peak tonnage in 1956.

[68] G. C. Allen, (ed.), *The Import Trade of the Port of Liverpool. Future Prospects* (1946), 74, W. J. Corlett and F. E. Hyde, 'Trade in Particular Commodities'.
[69] *Manchester Guardian*, 9 December 1930, 5, 'C.W.S. Tea Warehouse'.

Table 4

Traffic of the Manchester Ship Canal, 1894–1976

Year	Tonnage of exports	Tonnage of imports	Proportion of imports (%)	
			Volume	Value
1894	299,407	386,751	56·4	40·3
1895	494,862	592,581	54·5	31·9
1896	565,100	944,558	62·6	47·3
1897	616,842	1,053,637	62·0	52·0
1898	995,880	1,222,125	55·1	52·7
1899	993,751	1,435,417	59·1	54·5
1900	1,106,464	1,678,379	60·3	67·4
1901	1,012,836	1,671,997	62·3	64·3
1902	1,161,597	1,975,751	63·0	68·0
1903	1,385,700	2,168,936	61·0	68·6
1904	1,438,463	2,179,541	60·2	64·3
1905	1,748,238	2,244,872	56·2	63·1
1906	1,951,326	2,489,915	56·1	65·0
1907	2,354,659	2,573,125	52·2	64·4
1908	1,820,747	2,497,218	57·8	63·5
1909	1,810,312	2,480,453	57·8	66·5
1910	1,990,444	2,627,626	56·9	63·1
1911	2,032,415	2,862,255	58·5	60·0
1912	2,025,445	2,996,246	59·7	61·9
1913	2,254,968	3,202,250	58·7	62·7
1914	2,123,667	2,985,618	58·4	63·8
1915	2,343,061	2,772,893	54·2	70·0
1916	1,924,813	2,615,354	57·6	68·4
1917	1,577,023	2,266,301	59·0	65·2
1918	1,097,729	2,131,564	66·0	73·0
1919	1,076,187	2,237,433	67·5	66·9
1920	1,221,593	2,877,733	70·2	66·3
1921	883,138	2,234,331	71·7	60·0
1922	1,458,826	2,622,745	64·3	56·3
1923	1,957,079	3,150,569	61·7	59·5

Year	Tonnage of exports	Tonnage of imports	Proportion of imports (%)	
			Volume	Value
1924	1,696,665	3,484,950	67·3	63·5
1925	2,033,627	3,538,778	62·9	62·1
1926	1,493,397	5,040,383	77·1	67·2
1927	2,061,318	4,038,318	66·2	63·8
1928	2,067,610	3,953,706	65·7	66·7
1929	2,163,111	4,180,894	65·9	69·0
1930	1,895,749	4,198,970	68·9	72·4
1931	1,671,026	4,017,169	70·6	73·8
1932	1,582,766	3,526,782	69·0	72·8
1933	1,423,497	3,744,981	72·5	75·9
1934	1,523,555	4,253,264	73·6	77·3
1935	1,618,613	4,322,058	72·8	75·2
1936	1,507,108	4,637,638	75·5	77·0
1937	1,728,768	5,099,797	74·7	78·6
1938	1,499,252	4,704,530	75·8	77·9
1939	1,828,515	5,209,710	74·0	77·6
1940	1,912,620	5,975,907	75·8	
1941	1,611,691	6,098,124	79·1	
1942	1,885,742	5,976,222	76·0	
1943	1,775,865	5,511,878	75·6	
1944	1,876,790	5,625,409	75·0	
1945	2,050,003	4,227,106	67·3	
1946	1,517,110	3,992,975	72·5	56·0
1947	1,469,946	5,328,112	78·4	63·1
1948	2,004,942	6,117,390	75·3	66·4
1949	2,383,353	6,506,324	73·2	67·1
1950	2,779,443	6,968,519	71·5	65·3
1951	3,114,999	7,707,850	71·2	74·6
1952	4,095,740	7,611,772	65·0	70·6
1953	4,707,434	7,645,846	61·9	65·2
1954	4,909,000	11,308,528	69·7	69·9
1955	5,340,316	13,063,946	71·0	70·9
1956	5,328,631	13,040,439	71·0	68·1
1957	4,510,829	12,201,676	73·0	69·9

Year	Tonnage of exports	Tonnage of imports	Proportion of imports (%)	
			Volume	*Value*
1958	4,735,242	13,164,616	73·5	67·2
1959	4,963,042	13,532,241	73·2	66·6
1960	5,023,983	12,625,357	71·5	68·9
1961	4,969,218	9,884,761	66·5	67·3
1962	4,645,278	10,030,192	68·3	64·0
1963	4,184,673	10,879,456	72·2	66·7
1964	4,005,367	11,642,676	74·4	68·2
1965	4,177,000	10,932,000	72·4	66·4
1966	4,443,000	11,728,000	72·5	68·5
1967	4,131,000	12,000,000	74·4	66·9
1968	3,921,000	11,864,000	75·2	63·2
1969	3,764,000	11,814,000	75·8	61·8
1970	3,826,000	11,380,000	74·8	66·2
1971	5,356,000	10,602,000	66·4	58·4
1972	4,944,500	10,312,300	67·6	58·1
1973	5,192,600	10,505,300	66·9	60·9
1974	6,611,000	9,472,600	58·9	61·0
1975	6,101,000	7,746,000	55·9	59·4
1976	5,611,000	9,034,600	61·7	59·3

Source: Manchester Ship Canal Company, *Traffic Statistics, 1894–1964*, supplemented by National Ports Council, *Digest of Port Statistics*, 1966–73, and *Annual Digest of Port Statistics*, 1973–76, for the first two columns, converting tonnes of 2,205 lb (1,000 kg) for the years 1972–76 into tons of 2,240 lb; *Annual Statements of the Trade of the U.K.*, 1894–1974, for the statistics on which the last column is based.

4

The struggle for the raw cotton trade

The development of the cotton industry had made Manchester the industrial metropolis of the kingdom and Liverpool its leading shipping port as the greatest flow of textile exports ever known in the history of the world gathered strength in the early nineteenth century. The decline in the rate of expansion of the production, exports and profits of the cotton industry and its ancillary trades during the 1870s had provided the economic spur to the Ship Canal agitation. The prosperity previously generated by the cotton industry created the capital which was channelled into the Canal Company by local investors. The Ship Canal would, it was hoped, make Manchester into another Liverpool and derive both traffic and revenue from the staple trade of Lancashire. In 1885 Marshall Stevens estimated that the cotton industry would supply the Canal seven years after its opening with 7.6 per cent of its tonnage, both import and export, and with 12.7 per cent of its net revenue.[1] In the event in 1900 the industry supplied 11.5 per cent of the tonnage and 15.7 per cent of the net revenue. For the first nine years of operation the industry supplied more than half the value of the Canal's total trade and only from 1903 furnished less than half. During the twenty years 1894–1913 the Canal secured, however, only 41 per cent of the tonnage of raw cotton and only 46 per cent of that of piece-goods envisaged by Stevens because the cotton industry had increased its production by 34 per cent between 1885 and 1900 and because the bulk of its traffic

[1] M. Stevens, *The Commercial Aspects of the Manchester Ship Canal* (Manchester, Blacklock, 1891), 24, 26.

during the final Edwardian phase of expansion was retained by Liverpool. In particular Liverpool remained the centre of the import trade in raw cotton, although Manchester lay within carting distance of 80 per cent of the industry's spindleage and J. K. Bythell had spent the whole of his business career in the raw cotton trade. The Canal nevertheless succeeded in securing a larger share of the import trade in raw cotton than of the export trade in cotton manufactures because its use offered a greater proportionate saving on raw cotton than on piece-goods. It began to capture the trade in raw cotton only as that traffic entered upon its era of long-term decline: it handled its peak tonnage of textile exports in 1913 but its peak tonnage of cotton imports only in 1937.

Raw cotton was the object of an essentially seasonal trade lasting from September to April and remained much more important to the Ship Canal in value than in volume. From 1894 until 1952 it supplied the most valuable single import into the Port of Manchester. It was not, however, a bulk commodity and never contested the primacy in import tonnage held in succession by timber, grain and oil. Nor did it ever provide the major share of the total cotton imports into the country. Cotton imports reached their absolute peak level during the 1936–37 season and the peak of their relative importance in 1938–39, when Manchester handled 35 per cent of the total volume of retained imports. The comparative failure of the Ship Canal in this sphere was

Table 5

Proportion of the total imports of raw cotton into the U.K. entering the Port of Manchester, 1894–1938 (%)

Period	*Volume*	*Value*
1894–1913	15	17·9
1914–29	19	19·4
1930–38	32	27·9

Source: Manchester Ship Canal, *Traffic Statistics, 1894–1939. Annual Statements of Trade*, 1894–1938.

an almost inevitable consequence of the successful specialisation developed between Manchester and Liverpool since 1814 and of the invincible attraction exerted upon buyers by the greatest commodity market in the world.

Liverpool enjoyed all the advantages of an old-established, well known and reputable market which had become the universal depot for the cotton crops of the world and above all for that of the U.S.A. The ship owners and shippers of New Orleans had been closely linked to Liverpool since the 1820s by ties of mutual interest and were strongly prejudiced against the new route, preferring to ship in bulk by the customary channels and demanding higher freights on small consignments for Manchester.[2] Importing merchants in Liverpool feared a boycott of their stocks by local buying brokers if they shipped any cotton to Manchester for sale.[3] The Liverpool Cotton Association, registered in 1882 as a limited company, was dominated by the brokers and had reformed its practices after three successful corners of the cotton market in 1879, 1881 and 1883 had rallied support in industrial Lancashire to the Ship Canal agitation. The close links between brokers and spinners could not, however, be easily broken, based as they were on old-established connections, on family ties, on the extension of credit and on the investment of capital made during the 1880s in limited liability spinning companies. The vast bulk of cotton was bought by spinners in Liverpool either on the spot or for future delivery and both spot and future markets offered advantages to buyers unavailable elsewhere.

Manchester could not develop the import of cotton on a large scale until it had developed a market comparable to that of Liverpool. The creation of two markets forty miles apart for the same commodity was, however, as vast a task as the construction of the Canal itself or the creation of two separate shipping fleets. In 1894 Manchester had no market for cotton, no Cotton Exchange or Cotton Association, no importing merchants, buying brokers or jobbers, no warehouses for the storage of cotton and no banks specialising in the financing of

[2] B.O.D., 312–13, 26 April 1895.

[3] Manchester Cotton Association, *Minutes of the Board* (hereafter cited as 'M.C.A.B.'), 139–40, 23 September 1895.

cotton imports. Neither a spot market nor a futures market could be developed to foster the development of direct imports to Manchester. The development of a futures market in Manchester was the essential precondition to any substantial expansion of imports but remained precluded by the persistent opposition of Liverpool. That port retained its commanding position in the import of American cotton and its American futures contract served as the basis for the price of all non-American growths. Manchester could develop a futures market only by agreement with Liverpool to amend the form of its contract to permit cotton stored in Manchester to be tenderable against Liverpool future contracts. Manchester, however, lacked the large merchants necessary to undertake the daily sales of futures: it required enormous stocks of cotton in order to prevent the market from being cornered by outsiders and the price of all growths being thereby artificially raised. Until 1942 Liverpool consistently refused to modify its contract in order to prevent such speculative manoeuvres from without and to preserve the unity of its own great market, one and indivisible.

The spinners of Lancashire continued under such influences to take their custom to Liverpool. Their weekly visit to that port was sanctioned by a tradition of over sixty years and remained of great economic value to small spinners because of the wide range of choice available in the world's largest market for cotton. It was also an enjoyable social occasion, especially when combined with a weekend excursion to the Isle of Man. The dependence of spinners upon Liverpool was reinforced by the sharp decline in cotton prices, which amounted to 43 per cent between 1890 and 1895: that deflation encouraged spinners to reduce their stocks to the minimum, to replenish them only when necessary, to avoid making unnecessarily large purchases and thus to increase their reliance upon the Liverpool market and its warehousing facilities. The estimated proportion of cotton imports expected by the Canal had been revised downwards in 1891 from 74 per cent to 44 per cent. The saving on such direct imports was also revised downwards in 1894 from the £250,000 estimated in 1883 to £150,000, or from an anticipated 50 per cent of the cost via Liverpool to 30 per cent after precautionary

Barton Aqueduct: the empty tank before the diversion of the Bridgewater Canal, 1893 (*Manchester Central Library, Local History Collection*).

Barton Aqueduct in operation, 1894 (*Leech, op. cit., ii, 56*). The new aqueduct marked the beginning of the widest section of the Canal, which extended for three miles to the terminal docks and had a bottom width enlarged by 42 per cent from 120 ft to 170 ft, in order to permit the discharge of cargo without interfering with traffic. Upon that most important stretch of the Canal the task of replacing Brindley's aqueduct of 1760–61 presented the most formidable challenge to the engineer and enabled him to achieve his greatest triumph, replacing the engineering marvel of the eighteenth century by a technological masterpiece of the nineteenth. The first fixed canal aqueduct built in England was replaced by the first swing aqueduct ever to have been constructed. The new aqueduct was devised in principle by E. L. Williams in 1882 and was built by Handyside & Co. of Derby. Williams had devised the Anderton Lift (1875) on the Weaver Navigation and apparently hoped to duplicate that lift at Barton, building a high-level fixed aqueduct across the Ship Canal, with a lift at each end. He abandoned that impracticable scheme and devised a swinging aqueduct which proved to be his true masterpiece. It was only two-thirds the width of the fixed aqueduct but its tank was 7 ft deep rather than 4 ft 6 in., so making possible an increase of 18 in. in the draught of barges. It could be turned like a swing bridge by hydraulic power upon sixty-four rollers while a watertight breaking joint sealed the ends of both trough and canal. The swinging span weighed 1,450 tons, including 800 tons of water, and could be turned in the fast time of 2 min. 5 sec., leaving clear two 90 ft-wide spans of the Ship Canal. In the age of the motorway the same end of avoiding interference with traffic on the Ship Canal was effected by the construction (1957–60) of the Stretford high-level by-pass above the Canal. Two attempts were made to fill the aqueduct on 29 May and 14 June 1893 before success was achieved on 2 August, making possible the diversion of the Bridgewater Canal. The aqueduct was first crossed by barge on 17 August and was opened to traffic on 21 August (Leech, op. cit., ii, 173). The demolition of Brindley's aqueduct with its three supporting arches began in mid-September and was completed by 25 September, 'a small portion only of one of the pillars of the arches and the rock near the late entrance to Trafford Park remaining'. (*Manchester City News*, 7 October 1893, 5iv). One of the few descriptions of the aqueduct may be found in *Engineering*, 26 January 1894, 122–3.

reductions in both dock dues and railway rates reduced the competitive advantage of the Ship Canal.

The advantages of Liverpool over Manchester were greater in the import of American cotton than in the import of either Egyptian or Indian cotton. Those advantages were greatest of all in the re-export trade and least in the direct import trade on c.i.f. terms by spinners. Such direct imports comprised less than one-sixth of mill consumption and were diminishing under the pressure of Liverpool's competitive advantages in spot and future sales. They were, however, the main trade which the Canal Company could hope to attract to Manchester. The first imports of cotton to the new port were for spinners rather than for merchants: they arrived on 15 January 1894[4] at the very end of the cotton moving season of 1893–94, were carried from Galveston, the Texan rival of New Orleans, by the vessels of the Neptune Steam Navigation Company of Sunderland and presented no threat to Liverpool's monopoly of the cotton market. Bythell sought to persuade the Liverpool Cotton Association through the Master Cotton Spinners' Federation to include Manchester in the scope of its operations on equal terms, especially in relation to future contracts, but he found spinners unconvinced of the advantages of direct import and therefore he appointed traffic canvassers to work up the trade.[5] Manchester Charterers Ltd was established by the large investors of the Ship Canal Shareholders' Association led by Reuben Spencer (1830–1901), the chairman of Rylands & Sons Ltd, to establish a line of steamers between Manchester and the cotton ports of America but failed to secure enough support for the operations of the Neptune Steam Navigation Company[6] The Manchester Cotton Association Ltd was, however, incorporated on 28 November 1894 as a rival to the Liverpool Cotton Association, which had refused on 24 September to accept cotton stored in Manchester as tenderable against Liverpool future

[4] *Manchester Guardian*, 16 January 1894, 12iii; 17 January, 8v–vi.

[5] T.R.C., 136–7, 29 March 1894; 258–9, 14 June 1894.

[6] *Manchester City News*, 22 September 1894, 8vi. *Manchester Guardian*, 26 October 1894, 7i.

contracts.[7] That association was formed by spinners in co-operation with a few cotton merchants and with the approval of the Spinners' Federation in order to bypass the boycott of the Liverpool brokers: it was intended by Bythell as an essential preliminary to the establishment of a cotton market in Manchester and as a substitute for the Ship Canal Company in the function it had thitherto fulfilled in encouraging the direct import of cotton. The large American crop of ten million bales in 1894–95 offered the prospect of a golden harvest which was, however, reaped by Liverpool rather than by its new rival.[8] In 1894 and 1895 the Bridgewater Canal carried some 60 per cent more cotton than the Ship Canal from Liverpool to Manchester.

As the third cotton moving season approached, Bythell announced, in a circular to the charterers of American cotton steamers, a discount of 10 per cent on all cotton chartered with the Manchester option and carried at the same freight as to Liverpool.[9] None of the spinners' purchases of American cotton for the 1895–96 season was, however, booked for Manchester, because of a complete deadlock between charterers and merchants. The charterers of steamers loading at American ports refused to book freight for Manchester unless merchants were prepared to offer large quantities of cotton to start each steamer; the merchants would not offer cotton to buyers in England for shipment to Manchester unless they were certain of securing freight space. The directors of the Canal Company recognised the gravity of the situation and took immediate action in order to prevent the Ship Canal from being cut out of the import trade in cotton for a third successive season. On 27 September 1895 they authorised Bythell to ensure through Watts Watts & Co. of London and their correspondents at the American cotton ports a continuous supply of Manchester freight space day by day at the same rates as to Liverpool.[10] The decision was supported by an emergency meeting of the Manchester Cotton Association on 1 October and by a mass

7 B.O.D., 157–8, 28 September 1894; 169, 19 October 1894.
8 Ibid., 285–6, 22 March 1895; 331–2, 24 May 1895.
9 T.R.C., 85, 2 June 1895. B.O.D., 350, 21 June 1895; 371, 19 July 1895.
10 B.O.D., 414, 418, 27 September 1895; 5–7, 20 December 1895.

meeting of the cotton trade on 8 October: coupled with the completion of the port's first warehouses in 1895–96, it proved a decisive turning-point in the history of cotton imports into Manchester. The chartering of steamers by the Canal Company entailed a large short-term risk in the hope of long-term benefit and inspired Bythell to propose the establishment of an importing company in Manchester, in order to overcome the resistance of the Liverpool brokers and to sell Liverpool futures against imports to Manchester on a hedging basis.[11]

The policy of independent chartering was initiated too late in the season to produce much effect and was limited in its impact by the short crop of 1895 and by the consequent collapse of freights, so that the first four steamers made a heavy loss on the chartered rates.[12] The Neptune Steam Navigation Company was apparently offended by the undue preference given to other ship owners and withdrew its Manchester service in 1896 after three seasons in the cotton trade.[13] Bythell had, however, successfully established, despite immense difficulty, a direct service from New Orleans and Galveston to Manchester. He concluded that a shipping company was essential to secure the cotton trade, in order to ensure the necessary continuous daily supply of Manchester freight space at current rates during the cotton season.[14] His efforts stimulated emulation. Lamport & Holt undertook the import of Sea Island cotton from Florida via New York in November 1895, with the support of the fine spinners of Manchester.[15] The Larrinaga Line of Liverpool began a service of cotton steamers from Galveston to Manchester which was maintained for forty years from 1897.[16]

The policy of chartering was employed during three consecutive seasons with increasing success, despite the competitive reduction by

[11] Ibid., 466–7, 22 November 1895.

[12] Ibid., 433–5, 25 October 1895; 465–7, 22 November; 5–7, 18, 20 December 1895.

[13] *Manchester City News*, 13 February 1897, 5vii.

[14] B.O.D., 7, 20 December 1895.

[15] Ibid., 7–8, 10, 20 December 1895.

[16] *Manchester Guardian*, 31 July 1897, 5v. M.C.A.B., 13–14, 9 February 1937.

Liverpool of its dock dues on cotton.[17] Manchester rose in status from the fourth largest importer of cotton in 1894 and the third largest in 1895 to the second largest in 1896, while its share of cotton imports increased from 1.9 per cent in 1894–95 to 7 per cent in 1895–96 and to 9 per cent in 1896–97. By the time the 1898 season began not one of the lines linking the cotton ports of the U.S.A. with Manchester was being run at the sole risk of the Canal Company,[18] so encouraging Bythell to revive the idea of a Manchester Cotton Importing Syndicate Ltd.[19] Five years of continuous expansion raised cotton from the rank of the fourth largest import into the new port to that of the third in 1898. A slight recession in imports in 1899 was followed by the beginning of the Manchester Liners service from New Orleans and by a large increase during 1900, when raw cotton achieved its greatest relative significance in the import trade of the Canal,[20] supplying 8.8 per cent of the tonnage of imports but 47.3 per cent of their value and doubling Manchester's proportion of the total imports of cotton from 11 to 21 per cent. That increase in the imports of a valuable commodity helped to raise the unit value of imports above that of exports and so to establish an unusual pattern of commerce, which was maintained from 1900 until the war of 1939–45. Raw cotton never dominated the import traffic of the Canal as cotton manufactures dominated the export trade. It supplied the third largest tonnage after timber and grain during the six years 1898–1903 and was then surpassed in volume successively by imports of manufactured iron in 1904, by oil in 1907 and by stone setts in 1914, so receding to the sixth place whilst retaining its primacy in import values until 1952.

Manchester proved much more successful in importing raw cotton from Egypt than from the U.S.A. Egypt had replaced India in 1891 as the second largest source of supply of raw material to the mills of Lancashire: it supplied more cotton direct to Manchester than did the U.S.A. during the first two years of operation of the Ship Canal.

17 M.C.A.B., 224–5, 10 September 1896.
18 B.O.D., 448, 21 October 1898.
19 M.C.A.B., 20 October 1898, Minute No. 143.
20 Ibid., 6 September 1900, Minute No. 327.

Barton Lock gates, 1893 (*Leech, op. cit., ii, 34*). The 65 ft locks were modified in 1913–14 after the improvement of the Runcorn bend to permit the passage of vessels with a 63 ft beam.

Such was the achievement of James Knott (1855–1934)[21] of Newcastle, who maintained the service of the Prince Line from Manchester to Alexandria from 1894 against the most determined opposition of Liverpool ship owners led by the Moss Line.[22] Knott secured every support from the Canal Company, which supplied free towage, cheap labour and facilities for the barging of cargo to and from Liverpool. He also gained the custom of the medium fine spinners of Bolton, led by Horrockses and Tootal's. Bolton used Egyptian rather than American cotton and lay within the same magic radius of the twelve-mile carting limit as did Oldham but proved far stronger in support of the Canal. In 1894 the Prince Line secured the

[21] *The Times*, 9 June 1934, 19i.

[22] B.O.D., 164–5, 177, 19 October 1894; 192, 16 November; 219, 19 December 1894; 5, 20 December 1895.

invaluable contract for the shipment of piece-goods from Manchester to Alexandria and Syria.[23] In return its vessels secured to the new port a very good hold upon the Egyptian crop and carried the whole of the increment in cotton imports during 1895. The line extended the scope of its activity by bringing Egyptian cotton from Alexandria for transhipment to Hamburg and by entering from 1896 into the passenger trade.[24] The seal was set upon its success in 1898 by its entry into a working agreement with its rivals and its admission to the Egyptian Shipping Conference.[25] The conclusion of the first understanding between Manchester and Liverpool liners was a historic event and aroused no complaint until 1912 from the Egyptian shippers in Manchester, perhaps because it was not linked with any attempt to introduce the deferred rebate.

Manchester's share of the imports of Egyptian cotton rose from 21.4 per cent in 1895–96 to 33.6 per cent in 1899–1900, the sixth season of the Canal's operation. The growing imports of Egyptian cotton remained large enough to influence the general level of cotton imports into Manchester, accounting for 33 per cent of the increment in imports in 1899–1900 and for 45 per cent of the reduction in imports in 1909–10. Manchester's share of the Egyptian crop increased sharply at the expense of Liverpool in 1904–05, from 38 to 45 per cent as its share of direct American shipments sank. In 1905–06 Manchester first handled more of the retained imports of Egyptian cotton than Liverpool and in 1908–09 it first imported more Egyptian cotton than its older rival. During the twenty seasons from 1894–95 to 1913–14 Manchester handled 41.9 per cent of the retained imports of Egyptian cotton into the country but only 13 per cent of the retained imports of American. During seventeen of the thirty-four seasons from 1905–06 to 1938–39 Manchester handled more of the retained imports of Egyptian cotton than Liverpool.[26]

[23] *Manchester Guardian*, 22 February 1896, 5vii.

[24] B.O.D., 414–15, 27 September 1895. *Manchester Guardian*, 29 July 1896, 9vii; 8 September 9vi; 12 September 1896, 5vii.

[25] *Manchester Guardian*, 19 October 1898, 6vii; 20 October, 7ii–iii.

[26] In 1905–06, 1906–07, 1911–12, 1913–14, 1915–16, 1923–24 until 1929–30, and 1934–35 until 1938–39.

Thirty years of expansion in cotton shipments from Alexandria to Manchester culminated during the season of 1924–25, when Manchester imported its peak tonnage and its peak proportion of Egyptian cotton: those 234,297 bales supplied 33.6 per cent of its total cotton imports and 59.5 per cent of the total retained imports of Egyptian cotton into the U.K. That particular commerce secured to the port until the 1930s a higher proportion of the value of cotton imports than of their volume and extended Lancashire interests in Egypt, leading to the establishment of an Egyptian consulate in Manchester from 1928 until 1936.[27] The success of Manchester in attracting Egyptian cotton contrasted sharply with its comparative failure in diverting American cotton from Liverpool.

The Manchester Cotton Association (1894–1965) was established by spinners in order to encourage the large-scale purchase of cotton direct from America. It represented a new type of organisation in the history of the cotton industry in so far as it was intended to be permanent rather than temporary. Even with only 33 per cent of the industry's spindleage it represented a capital of £33 million and 'the most powerful association of buyers the world has ever seen'.[28] Nevertheless it had undertaken the almost impossible task of transferring to Manchester the largest single trade of Liverpool. It found that in order to fulfil its function it had to acquire the mercantile support and expertise, the financial backing and the statistical information possessed by the Liverpool Cotton Association: it had to prepare contract forms modelled on those used in Liverpool, voluminous by-laws, a black list of American shippers and regular weekly returns of sales and stocks. At the first meeting of the shareholders the Association elected its moving spirit, J. K. Bythell, as its vice-president.[29] From 20 April 1895 it published with the financial

[27] M.C.A.B., 33, 10 August 1926; 193, 17 April 1928; 22–3, 11 February 1936.

[28] Manchester Ship Canal Company, *Report of the Directors*, 28 February 1895, 4, J. K. Bythell.

[29] Manchester Cotton Association, *Minutes of Shareholders' Meetings*, 26 March 1895, 2.

help of the Canal Company a weekly journal, *Cotton*, in order to further the interests of the Canal.[30] It was hampered, however, by the understandable determination of the Canal Company to maintain the level of transit rates between Liverpool and Manchester in defiance of the expectation of spinners of cheaper transit to their mills. Only a limited degree of support from the industry was secured as the membership of the Association rose during the first decade of its existence to represent 43.5 per cent of the total spindleage.[31] Its operations were also impeded by a lack of support from merchants, by the divorce between buyers and sellers and by that between merchants and brokers. The Association proved more successful in providing for arbitration through its appeal committees, which were first established in 1895 for American cotton and for Egyptian cotton and were supplemented by an Indian Appeal Committee in 1903 and by a Waste Appeal Committee in 1906. The board of directors declined, however, to form a Spinners' Arbitration Committee, in order to avoid encroaching upon the province of the Master Cotton Spinners' Federation.[32] The Association achieved some success in inducing the fine spinners of Bolton, Leigh and Manchester to make their future purchases of Sea Island cotton on c.i.f. terms deliverable at the Port of Manchester.[33] Those imports were high in value but represented only 0.7 per cent of the total exports of U.S. cotton to Great Britain.

The Association's limited degree of success inspired efforts to supplement its activity by the foundation of an importing company, which was proposed on five separate occasions, in 1895, 1898, 1902, 1904 and 1908, before its eventual establishment in 1923.[34] Such a speculative venture might have helped to create a spot market in

[30] B.O.D., 256–7, 259, 15 February 1895; 313, 26 April 1895.

[31] M.C.A.B., 114, 5 October 1905.

[32] Ibid., 19, 8 October 1908.

[33] Ibid., 106–9, 24 June 1895.

[34] M.C.A.B., 2 October 1902, Minute No. 128, E. Stansfield. B.O.D., 57, 30 December 1904; 65, 13 January 1905. M.C.A.B., 72, 5 January 1905; 82–3, 2 March 1905. Manchester Ship Canal Company, *Report of the Directors*, 13 February 1908, 5.

Manchester but would have involved shareholders in direct competition with the skill and capital of the cotton brokers of Liverpool and could not secure sufficient backing either within the Association or within the Canal Company. The association also tried from 1898 to establish a spot market in Manchester and thrice sought to create a formal market such as had emerged in the grain and timber trades. The establishment of a Cotton Bureau in October 1901 for sales of cotton failed to secure enough support from spinners to make it viable[35] and provoked only a determined effort in 1901–03 by the Liverpool ship owners, led by the Harrison Line, to drive Manchester steamers off the berths of the American cotton ports. The attempt in 1908 to re-establish such a Sales Bureau was opposed by both merchants and brokers, since it would institutionalise competition amongst themselves and would lie outside their exclusive control.[36] The Cotton Sale Room was opened on 23 November 1908 but proved only a moderate success,[37] so that imports to Manchester continued until 1927 to be largely c.i.f. The establishment of a futures market was far more difficult than that of a spot market but was repeatedly considered[38] and was discussed at ten special meetings of the Association's directors between 19 April 1910 and 20 June 1911, when the proposal to form a Manchester Cotton Association (Futures Section) 1910 Ltd in the interests of the spinners foundered upon the deep differences between the merchant-directors and the spinner-directors of the Association: the large merchants withheld support for fear of a boycott of their trade by Liverpool brokers.[39]

The Great War reduced Manchester's competitive capacity as a cotton port by increasing the cost of labour, materials and Canal dues but was followed by an increase in imports of American cotton into Manchester to an all-time peak in 1919–20, when U.S. cotton formed

[35] M.C.A.B., 18 April 1901, Minute No. 518; 18 July 1901, Minute No. 542; 149, 1 October 1903; 80, 16 February 1905.

[36] Ibid., 150–1, 4 February 1908; 174–7, 17 March 1908.

[37] Ibid., 29–32, 19 November 1908; 53–4, 19 January 1909; 131, 21 December 1909; 145–6, 1 February 1910.

[38] In 1894, 1897, 1902, 1906, 1907, 1909, 1910–11, 1914, 1915, 1917, 1918, 1928, 1929–30, 1932, 1934, 1935 and 1937.

[39] M.C.A.B., 41–2, 3 October 1910; 115–18, 18 July 1911.

Irlam Locks, 1892 (*Manchester Central Library, Local History Collection*). At Irlam, or Irwelham, 'the village on the winding stream', the locks were built in two-and-a-quarter years (1890–92) and were excavated in water-laden soil, requiring about 10,000 tons of cement to provide a solid foundation. The duplicate locks, 600 ft × 65 ft and 350 ft × 45 ft, raised vessels by 16 ft in what became from 1909 the largest single lift on the Canal. Those locks were the widest set on the Canal, which broadened out to 370 ft, in order to accommodate the five adjacent sluices: the other interior locks at Latchford, Barton and Mode Wheel had duplicate locks of the same size but only four sluices. The Canal was equipped with a total of thirty large flood sluices and eighty lock sluices. The flood sluices were necessary to cope with the rainfall collected from a watershed of 500,000 acres formed by the basins of the Irwell and Mersey: the lock sluices were designed simply to transfer water from one lock to another in order to avoid wastage. All used the self-balancing roller gate patented in 1874 by Francis G. M. Stoney (1837–97) and built by Ransome & Rapier of Ipswich under the management of Stoney from 1887. The rolling sluice made possible easy movement of the 32 ton gates and was popularised by its use on the Ship Canal. It was adopted by Sir William Willcocks (1852–1932) for the 140 under sluices and the forty upper sluices of the Aswan Dam (1898–1902) on the Upper Nile. Beyond the lock can be seen the hydraulic power house, which also supplied power to the coal hoists at Partington, one-and a-half miles distant. The Irlam section of the Canal was surveyed in the *Manchester Guardian*, 2 December 1893, 9iv–vi, and in the *Minutes of the Proceedings of the Institution of Civil Engineers*, vol. 131, 1897–98. Part i, 53–7, W. O. E. Meade-King. Obituaries of Stoney may be found in ibid., vol. 130, 1896–97, Part iv, 316–18, and in *The Engineer*, 27 August 1897, 207.

79 per cent of the total volume of cotton imports into Manchester but represented only 21 per cent of the retained imports of American cotton into the U.K. The formation in 1923 of the Manchester Raw Cotton Co. Ltd under the auspices of the Canal Company helped to increase the volume of cotton imports into Manchester by 43 per cent in 1923–24. Liverpool maintained, however, its dominant position in the import of the American staple and monopolised also the import of cotton from Brazil and the Sudan: it derived particular benefit from the increased import of raw cotton from the Empire under the influence of the British Cotton Growing Association, established in 1902, the Empire Cotton Growing Corporation, founded in 1921, and the Lancashire Cotton Corporation Ltd, registered in 1929.[40] As the cotton kingdom of the U.S.A. expanded to its maximum acreage and the Lancashire cotton industry reached the peak of its spindleage the Manchester Cotton Association finally established on 19 December 1927 central selling rooms in the Royal Exchange, under the control of its merchant members, to serve as a spot cotton market in Manchester,[41] with the aid of the Canal Company. The move proved successful enough to provoke an immediate boycott by the Liverpool Cotton Association which was maintained for twenty-seven months.[42] Imports of raw cotton to Manchester increased for four successive seasons from 1928–29 after the Association increased its membership to represent 54 per cent of the industry's spindles[43] and the Canal Company reduced its rates in 1927–29 to the pre-war level.[44] Manchester benefited especially from the increased import of Indian cotton: it imported more Indian cotton than Liverpool from 1929–30 and handled its peak proportion of the retained imports of Indian cotton in 1930–31, when it imported 75.3 per cent of the total imports thereof. The influx of Indian cotton increased after the bilateral agreement of 1933 linked the use of Indian cotton in Lancashire mills to the export of Lancashire

40 Ibid., 116, 12 July 1927; 103–4, 11 June 1929; 68, 9 July 1935.
41 Ibid., 149–51, 22 November 1927; 154, 13 December 1927.
42 Ibid., 177–8, 28 February 1928; 171–2, 8 April 1930.
43 Ibid., 75, 11 January 1927; 91–2, 13 April 1927.
44 Ibid., 58, 13 November 1928; 120, 3 September 1929.

goods to India: it supplied some compensation for the decline in the imports of Egyptian cotton from their peak level of 1924–25 as Combined Egyptian Mills Ltd of Bolton deserted Manchester for Liverpool.[45]

Manchester's imports of Indian cotton reached their absolute peak in the climactic season of 1936–37, when they supplied 41 per cent of its total imports of cotton. During that season imports rose to a record level, which first surpassed the peak of 1919–20 and was never attained again. Thus Manchester's imports of cotton reached their maximum twenty-five years after the national peak of 1912: those imports represented 5 per cent of the tonnage of imports in 1937 but 26 per cent of their value. During the season of 1936–37 1,071,223 bales were imported, representing 33.3 per cent of total imports, 71 per cent of retained imports of Indian cotton and 53 per cent of imports of Egyptian cotton but only 34.3 per cent of imports of American cotton. The U.S.A. reached its all-time peak level of cotton production in 1937 and enabled Manchester to handle its peak proportion of cotton imports, especially from America. In 1938–39 the port imported 35 per cent of total imports but 46 per cent of total imports of the American staple. The record imports of 1937 raised the Manchester Cotton Association to the summit of its importance and inspired friendly negotiations with the Liverpool Cotton Association on the acceptability of Manchester cotton against Liverpool future contracts. The fundamental principle of acceptability failed only narrowly to secure approval in a poll of the membership of the Liverpool Association.[46]

After the futures market was closed with effect from 31 March 1941, so making impossible the transfer of trade from one port to the other, the Liverpool Cotton Association in 1942 accepted Manchester cotton as tenderable against Liverpool contracts,[47] so formally fulfilling a desire cherished in Manchester for forty-eight years. The year 1942 was, however, one of deep war-induced depression in the

45 Ibid., 173–4, 12 July 1932; 182, 13 September; 198, 8 November; 2, 13 December 1932.

46 Ibid., 92, 14 December 1937.

47 Ibid., 67–8, 8 December 1942.

cotton industry, reducing the consumption of cotton to the level of 1869 and the value of exports of cotton manufactures to the lowest level since the crisis year of 1862. The Liverpool cotton market did not re-open until 1954, when Manchester's imports had receded to the level of 1899. The Manchester Cotton Association was wound up in 1965 when the cotton imports of the port had declined to their original low level before the great upward leap of 1896 and tobacco had replaced cotton in the warehouses of Trafford Park. Raw cotton had ceased to be the most valuable single import into the U.K. in 1874 and into Liverpool in 1926 but continued to supply the Port of Manchester with its most valuable import until 1952, as direct purchase increased with the growth in the size of firms. The failure to capture more of the import of raw cotton proved a blessing in disguise: it insulated the traffic of the Canal from the cyclical depressions inseparable from 'the highest and most nervous form of life in the kingdom of commerce'[48] and ensured that its trade would not share the fate of the cotton industry.

[48] W. H. Mills, *Sir Charles W. Macara, Bart.: a Study of Modern Lancashire* (Manchester, Sherratt, 1917), 49.

5

The development of the export trades

Manchester became more important as a port of import than as one of export from the time of the opening of the Canal to traffic. The city served as the main market for the country's leading export industry but its shippers remained in general firmly linked by mutual interest to the ship-owning lines of Liverpool through the institution of the deferred rebate which was granted on exports and not on imports. The cotton industry had reduced its contribution to the export trade since 1831 and diverted only a portion of its traffic to the Ship Canal. The exports of the new port did not develop on the same pattern or to the same extent as its imports. They comprised much smaller parcels than imports and remained more limited in volume and in range, being dominated in volume by coal but in value by cotton manufactures.

Exports were surpassed by imports in volume from 1894 and in value from 1897 so that Manchester acquired a permanent import surplus which increased during the following forty years. Until 1899 exports expanded more rapidly in volume than imports but more slowly in value. They did not experience a gradual increase in value so much as a sharp rise during 1895 with the advent of the export of piece-goods. Then they suffered a recession by 16 per cent in value in 1896–97, while imports continued to expand until 1901. In volume they reached in 1907 a pre-war peak which was not surpassed until 1949: they reached an absolute peak in 1955 before the Suez crisis, whilst imports reached a peak level in 1959. In value they continued to expand after 1955 but they had achieved their largest share of U.K. exports in 1919, while imports did not reach their peak proportion of

Table 6

Share of the main exports in the total export trade of the Canal, 1894–1913

Commodity	*Volume* (%)	*Value* (%)
Cotton manufactures	13·12	69·22
Coal	51·86	0·94
Salt	8·69	0·19
Machinery	3·17	10·6
Total	28,089,455 tons	£238,131,147

Note: The statistics for salt refer to the years 1909–13 and not to 1894–1913.
Source: Manchester Ship Canal, *Traffic Statistics, 1894–1913. Annual Statements of Trade*, 1894–1913.

Table 7

Mean annual rates of increase in the traffic of the Canal, 1894–1959 (%)

	Value of exports	*Value of imports*
1894–1919	10·16	26·44
	Tonnage of exports	*Tonnage of imports*
1894–1959	4·5	6·04

Source: Manchester Ship Canal, *Traffic Statistics, 1894–1964. Annual Statements of Trade*, 1894, 1919

the nation's imports until 1956.

Until the beginning of the container revolution in 1966 exports remained more liable than imports to suffer from cyclical depression, declining in volume below the level of the preceding year in thirty of the seventy years between 1894 and 1964, while imports underwent similar recessions in only twenty-three such years. In 1899 exports suffered their first slight recession in volume, while imports did not experience such a setback until 1901. From 1899 exports expanded more slowly in volume than imports and so departed from the national trend of exports expanding faster than imports. The unit value of exports also sank below that of imports from 1900 until the war of 1939–45 so that the Port of Manchester acquired a structure of trade resembling that of a colonial port, comprising relatively dear imports and relatively cheap exports.

In order to encourage exports the Manchester Association of Importers and Exporters was established on 26 February 1908 to negotiate as a united body with the conferences of ship owners. The Association brought together representatives of the cotton industry, the machinery and iron trades, the chemical industry, the produce trade and the Ship Canal Company. It formed sections on the model of the Chamber of Commerce for Australia and for the Persian Gulf in 1908 and for Egypt in 1911:[1] it sought in every way to remove the disabilities imposed upon the Port of Manchester by merchants as well as by ship owners, devoting most effort to the development of exports. Its main achievement may have been negative rather than positive in so far as it curbed independent action by ship owners: it did not succeed in its efforts to secure the establishment of new steamship services either to the Plate in 1908 or to China in 1912. Two more sections were formed in 1916 to consolidate trade between Britain and two of its wartime allies, Italy and Russia.[2] In 1918 the Australian section was enlarged to include South Africa, while the Egyptian

[1] Manchester Association of Importers and Exporters, *Minutes*, 49, 29 April 1908; 90, 16 September 1908; 8–9, 20 December 1911.

[2] Ibid., 174–5, 18 October 1916; 185–6, 24 October; 191–2, 29 November; 204–5, 18 December 1916.

section was extended to the Levant.[3] The Association published twenty-eight admirable annual reports (1908–35), all prepared by its secretary, J. S. McConechy (1859–1936).[4] It provided a useful ancillary to the Chamber of Commerce and was transformed in 1935 into one of its sections. The Port of Manchester Committee was established on 11 July 1935 as a standing committee of the Chamber of Commerce in order to bring together the suppliers and the users of port facilities. That committee prepared four valuable reports on the traffic of the port[5] as well as a widely distributed booklet for schools.[6] It also considered the possibility of establishing an export cargo clearing house to collect information on pending shipments and to provide the necessary shipping[7] before its activities were suspended by the outbreak of war.

The export traffic of the Canal was dominated in volume by the bulky commodities of coal and salt but in value by cotton manufactures and machinery. Coal supplied the largest tonnage of exports from 1894 until 1951 and the second largest tonnage after oil from 1951 to 1961. Coal also supplied bunker fuel to steamships leaving the docks so that its importance was under-recorded in the statistics of export. Coal exports did not arouse the enthusiasm of Bythell until 1907 because they could not bear a high toll and were not expected ever to grow to large dimensions, as at one of the great coal ports. Indeed, annual shipments averaged 728,300 tons from 1894 to 1913,

3 Ibid., 274, 7 October 1918; 282, 17 October 1918.

4 *Manchester Guardian*, 21 December 1936, 11iv.

5 Manchester Chamber of Commerce, Port of Manchester Committee, *Minutes*, 19–32, 12 December 1935, 'Survey of Commodities Tending to use Port Facilities other than those offered by the Port of Manchester'; 14–19, 16 November 1937, and 8–13, 12 January 1938, [H. C. N. Ellis], 'Memorandum on Direct Shipments from Australia to the Port of Manchester'; 25–35, 16 November 1937, 'The Port of Manchester and the Engineering Industry'; 61–3, 1 December 1938, 'Transport of Provisions from Dublin and Interior Irish Stations to Manchester and Interior English Stations'.

6 The Port of Manchester Committee of the Manchester Chamber of Commerce, *The Inland Port of Manchester. Its Ships and their Cargoes* (1938, 37 pp.).

7 Manchester Chamber of Commerce, Port of Manchester Committee, *Minutes*, 4, 15 February 1939.

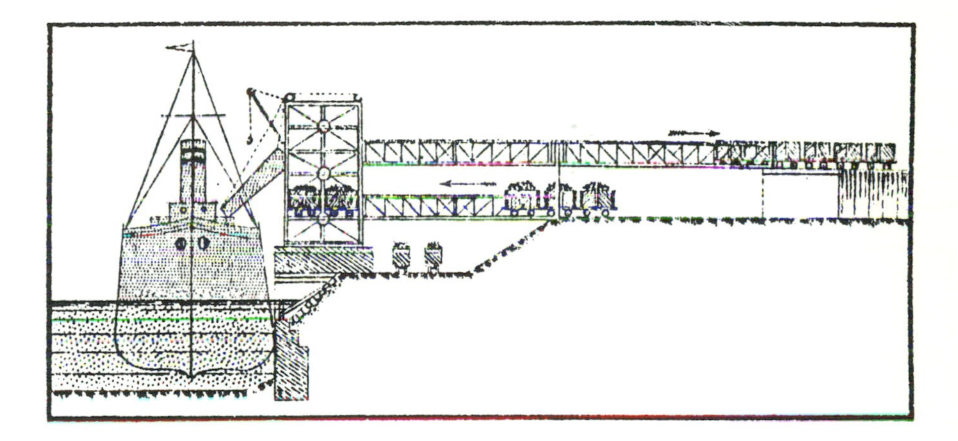

The Partington coaling basin, 1894 (*Manchester Central Library, Local History Collection*). The widening of the Ship Canal to 250 ft for three-quarters of a mile gave room for vessels to lie upon each side of the basin and for two ships to pass in the middle. The berths were equipped with four coal hoists which were soon increased in number to six. They were operated by hydraulic machinery supplied by Sir W. G. Armstrong Mitchell & Co., which became Armstrong-Whitworth in 1897 and so strengthened the Newcastle–Manchester axis. The technique of mechanical handling was applied first to coal, then to grain and oil and finally to all palletised and containerised cargo, making cargo handling a capital-intensive operation in the Port of Manchester whilst it remained a labour-intensive occupation in Liverpool.

or only one-seventh of the five million tons per annum expected by Adamson in 1883: at their peak level in 1907 coal exports amounted to 1.46 million tons.

An export station had been created at very great expense at Partington, eight miles to the west of Manchester and just beyond the confluence of the Mersey with the Ship Canal, with hydraulic tipping machinery on the Tyneside pattern supplied by Armstrong-Mitchell of Newcastle. Partington became the nearest port to the coalfields of Lancashire and brought the collieries of South Yorkshire, especially Barnsley, thirty miles nearer to the sea. The export trade languished, however, for the first nine months of the Canal's existence while the Bridgewater Canal carried during 1894 four times as much coal as the Ship Canal. Lancashire coal had thitherto been consumed mainly within the shire and was comparatively unknown in outside markets, where it could not sell for bunker purposes in competition with the steam coal of Cardiff. Lancashire collieries had developed close links with Liverpool and with the railway port of Garston, which remained the great competitor of Partington and was favoured by its creator, the London & North Western Railway.[8] The carriage of coal from Yorkshire did not develop until the railway companies settled through rates and the Canal Company agreed to accept only a modest share of the toll and terminal.[9] Such rates were arranged first by the Manchester Sheffield & Lincolnshire Railway in September 1894 and then by the Midland Railway, its partner in the Cheshire Lines Committee, in November 1894.[10] Thenceforward the collieries of Barnsley became a main contributor to the mineral traffic of the Ship Canal. The prospect of the export trade via the Canal encouraged the merger of collieries in Bolton and Wigan but did not prevent the relative decline of coal mining in Lancashire.[11]

Five years of increasing coal exports culminated in 1898, when a miners' strike in South Wales, coupled with the completion of the

[8] B.O.D., 468, 22 November 1895; 13, 20 December 1895.

[9] Ibid., 167, 19 October 1894.

[10] Ibid., 216–17, 19 December 1894.

[11] *Northern Finance and Trade*, 15 December 1897, 494; 2 February 1898, 97, J. Warburton, 'Collieries in Lancashire'.

Lancashire & Yorkshire Railway link, helped to double exports from Manchester. The depression of 1901 was the first serious check to the sustained expansion of Canal traffic and was caused largely by a decline in coal exports, as coal prices remained above their level at the great shipping ports. Exports rose sharply in 1903 under the stimulus of a temporary demand from America and doubled between 1904 and 1907, necessitating regular annual extensions to the installations at Partington.[12] Coal exports reached the peak of their relative importance during the fourteen years 1898–1911, when they supplied 53.4 per cent of the total tonnage of exports. They reached their absolute peak in 1907, when a prolonged colliery strike in Yorkshire blocked the eastern ports with fleets of steamers waiting to load and diverted some of the traffic in Yorkshire coal to Partington, raising exports of coal to their all-time maximum six years before the pre-war national peak of 1913 but supplying only 2.3 per cent of the total volume of British coal exports. During 1907 coal supplied 94 per cent of the increment in export tonnage, which soared to the highest level it was to reach before 1949, and the Canal Company sought to turn Ellesmere Port into a bunkering port, especially for steamers in the Eastern and Australasian trade, so as to make Manchester rather than Liverpool the last port of loading.[13]

In 1908 coal production in Lancashire began to decline from the all-time maximum reached in 1907, six years before the national peak of 1913, and coal exports via the Canal declined sharply by 46 per cent, accounting for 86 per cent of the loss of export tonnage, reducing total exports by 23 per cent and precipitating a serious recession in the traffic of the Canal. Coal exports had expanded faster than other exports since 1894, had supplied 65.5 per cent of the increment in export tonnage between 1894 and 1907, and had reduced the average unit value of exports below that of imports from 1900. They remained relatively stable after the depression of 1908 as Manchester reverted to its position as a marginal exporter. The national miners'

[12] B.O.D., 147–8, 7 November 1902; 41–3, 2 December 1904; 48–50, 16 December 1904; 131, 19 May 1905; 334, 3 August 1906; 424–5, 15 March 1907.
[13] Ibid., 14, 6 September 1907.

strike of 1912 reduced coal shipments via the Canal by 10 per cent but caused a much slighter recession in traffic than that of 1901. In only two years after 1911, in 1918 and 1923, did coal again supply more than half the tonnage of exports. The import of coal via the Canal as distinct from its export took place only under exceptional circumstances and was significant only in 1926, in 1941–47 and in 1951–57. In 1926 the miners' strike reversed the flow of coal along the Canal and led to the import of 1.22 million tons, which accounted for 81 per cent of the increment in import tonnage and raised the traffic of the Canal to a level exceeded only in 1937.

The coal trade turned Partington into a great railway depot and attracted to the district a range of other trades, beginning with the steel industry. The Partington Steel & Iron Company, a subsidiary of Pearson & Knowles of Warrington, was encouraged by the availability of coal to build a steelworks in 1910–14.[14] The works was opened in time for the full employment created by the Great War, was absorbed by the Lancashire Steel Corporation in 1930 and dominated the economic life of Irlam until its closure in 1976.[15] From 1913 its demands stimulated imports of ore via the Canal, which surpassed the volume of manufactured iron imports from 1944 and rose in status from the fourth largest import in 1928 to the second in 1954. A gasworks was opened at Partington in 1929 by Manchester Corporation. Then the oil and chemical trades developed from the 1950s as the staple function of coal was inherited by its fellow hydrocarbon oil, creating from a humble nucleus an industrial complex comparable to that of Stanlow.

Salt supplied another bulk export similar to coal but was even cheaper and paid only half the toll to the Canal Company paid by coal. It had been one of the first commodities carried along the Canal from the country's primary source of supply in the Cheshire wiches after the foundation in 1892 of Saltport at the confluence of the

[14] Ibid., 362, 11 February 1910; 414–18, 22 July 1910; 90, 24 October 1913; 304, 4 December 1914.

[15] P. McGeown, *Heat the Furnace Seven Times More: An Autobiography* (London, Hutchinson, 1967, with introduction by Asa Briggs).

Weaver with the Canal.[16] Shipments along the Weaver had served as one of the mother-trades of Liverpool but had declined sharply from their peak volume of 1881 as the chemical industry of Northwich developed. They were carried by the barges of the Salt Union, established in 1888, and were delivered in Liverpool at an inclusive price, benefiting by a reduction in the Weaver tolls on salt by one-sixth in 1894. Thus Saltport was bypassed and failed to fulfil the hopes of its founders that it would supply back-loads to vessels using the Canal: it was abandoned in favour of Runcorn after 1895 and its jetty was dismantled in 1905.[17]

Salt exports developed via the Ship Canal only after the Salt Union agreed in November 1895 to deliver salt f.o.b. ship at Manchester at the same price as at Liverpool.[18] Those shipments raised the port in status from the eighth largest exporter of salt in 1895 to that of the third in 1896 and increased in importance from the fourth largest export in 1895–98 to the third after coal and textiles in 1899. They remained relatively stagnant between 1902 and 1908 but doubled in amount between 1908 and 1913 after the Salt Union established in 1909–11 a large new works on the Ship Canal at Weston, near Runcorn, producing 125,000 tons per annum for the Calcutta market.[19] Salt exports increased faster than those of any other commodity to reach their apogee in 1913 when the Port of Manchester displaced Middlesbrough as an exporter of salt and ranked second only to Liverpool. Salt even replaced textiles as the second largest export of the Canal in 1914–16 and in 1919–24. Although it was not a very remunerative commodity it provided a very useful cargo, enabling steamers to leave fully instead of partly laden, attracting others away from Liverpool and supplying ballast.

Exports of chemicals were slow to develop in place of the raw material of salt, although the United Alkali Co. Ltd had extended its plant at Wiggs Works on the Canal near Runcorn in 1897–99 for the

[16] T.L.P.C., 81, 17 June 1892; 96, 8 July 1892. *Manchester Guardian*, 16 December 1892, 5vii, 'Saltport'.

[17] B.O.D., 115, 14 April 1905.

[18] Ibid., 372–3, 19 July 1895; 13–14, 20 December 1895.

[19] Ibid., 261–3, 28 May 1909; 295–303, 1 October 1909.

manufacture of fertiliser from phosphate imported from America.[20] Those exports began to expand from 1912 and increased markedly from 1925 after the establishment of seven chemical works in Trafford Park between 1912 and 1925, stimulated by the wartime exclusion of German products from the British market. They replaced salt as the source of the second largest tonnage of exports after coal from 1925 to 1941. They reached their peak tonnage in 1955 but regained from coal their second place in exports from 1962 as the manufacture of petrochemicals expanded. Such traffic greatly enhanced the value of exports and the revenues of the Canal Company by replacing the humblest of commodities by one of the most valuable.

Textiles and machinery contributed value to the export trade where coal and salt supplied bulk: together they accounted for eight-tenths of the value of the Canal's exports during its first twenty years of operation. Textiles were also important in mere tonnage: they provided the second largest export after coal from 1895 until 1914, when they were displaced by salt. They ranked third from 1914 to 1924 and fourth from 1925 to 1930, being surpassed during the world economic depression by oil in 1931 and by petrol in 1932, when they were relegated to the sixth place. In the export of cotton manufactures Manchester succeeded in capturing much more of the trade in yarn than of that in piece-goods and thus competed with Hull more than with Liverpool. The freight on yarn was reduced much more than that on cloth, and that on yarn shipped to the Continent was cut sharply by 38.5 per cent after the opening of the Ship Canal. During 1894 Manchester surpassed Hull in the volume of its yarn exports and ranked second to Liverpool, handling 17 per cent of the total quantity exported from Britain and almost half the quantity exported from Liverpool. The trade had, however, been in slow decline from its maximum level of 1884 and lay largely outside the control of Liverpool, unlike the trade in piece-goods. The export of cotton textiles was a much more valuable trade than that in yarn,

[20] Ibid., 293, 30 July 1897; 417, 15 July 1898; 453, 4 November 1898.

The Thelwall Brook syphon, 1893 (*Manchester Central Library, Local History Collection*). The cast-iron syphon laid below the surface of the bed of the Canal in order to carry the waters of the Thelwall Brook northwards into the river Mersey.

being large, regular and increasing in volume, but was largely monopolised by the powerful conference lines of Liverpool, Glasgow and London. In order to enter that trade Manchester had either to attract non-conference vessels or to persuade the conference lines to send ships up the Canal. Outside ship owners were tempted to use Manchester as a Cave of Adullam only in time of depression, while conference lines were not prepared to use a route which offered no additional cargo or higher freights to compensate for the delay and inconvenience of an inland voyage. Their opposition was overcome only after Bythell had become chairman of the Canal Company and the waterway had been dredged, in August 1894, to its full depth of 26 ft.

The first steamer from Manchester to pass through the Suez Canal and to begin direct trade with Asia was the *Gorji* of the Persian Gulf Steamship Company, which sailed on 30 January 1894 with Manchester goods for the Gulf.[21] The Liverpool lines forced that company off the Manchester berth by halving freights and then they restored them to their former level. The first attempt to link Manchester direct to its largest single overseas market in India was made in February by D. & C. MacIver of Liverpool, who failed to raise £150,000 in Manchester in order to establish a Manchester & Liverpool Steamship Company on the route to Karachi and Bombay. From August 1894 Bythell undertook active negotiations through his old friends amongst the three hundred Hindu merchants of Bombay to secure the carriage of piece-goods to that port for the Canal. The Bombay Native Merchants' Piece Goods Association had procured within a year of its foundation in 1882 a reduction in net freights by 37 per cent and so secured a control over shipping charges possessed by no other importers: it determined to encourage the competition of Manchester with Liverpool in order to secure a further reduction and so performed the function which Manchester shippers dared not assume. Furness Withy & Co. Ltd decided to form a new company, the Manchester Bombay & General Navigation Co. Ltd, and made a tender to the Native Merchants' Association for the

[21] *Manchester Guardian*, 1 February 1894, 8vii.

years 1895 and 1896 in competition with the Clan, City, Anchor and Hall lines, which had been united since 1886 in the Bombay Conference.[22] The acceptance of that tender on 6 November disturbed the conference lines deeply, compelled them for the first time to take the Canal seriously and encouraged Bythell to extend his efforts to the Calcutta and China trades.[23] The conference failed to secure any reduction in the railway rates between Manchester and Liverpool and then succeeded in buying off its potential competitor for a reputed £11,000 after the Native Merchants' Association had tried to beat down rates even further.[24]

The Bombay contract was signed on 29 December 1894 with the conference lines rather than with the new London company. It was concluded for only one year instead of for the usual two and reduced the through rate by only 10 per cent instead of by the expected 20 per cent but provided for the loading of at least three steamers per month in Manchester.[25] Charles Cayzer (1848–1916), the chairman of the Clan Line and of the Bombay Conference, also promised Bythell to try to get Karachi goods for the Ship Canal and to discharge Calcutta cargo at Manchester after London.[26] The new Manchester and Bombay Company was diverted from the trade to India and explored in succession the possibility of a service to the Levant, to the Channel Islands and to Montreal.[27] The first conference liners to leave Manchester for Bombay were the *Hispania* of the Anchor Line on 6 January 1895 and the *Clan Drummond* of the Clan Line on 22 January.[28] The *City of Dublin* was the first vessel of the City Line to

[22] B.O.D., 170–1, 178, 19 October 1894.

[23] Ibid., 190–1, 195, 16 November 1894; 210, 7 December; 213–14, 19 December 1894.

[24] *Proceedings of the Manchester Chamber of Commerce, 1894–1899, Committees* (M8/3/2), Shipping Committee, 358, 25 April 1898, 'Freights on Manchester Cottons to the Far East'.

[25] T.R.C., 65–7, 4 January 1895. B.O.D., 233–6, 18 January 1895.

[26] B.O.D., 371–2, 19 July 1895; 413, 27 September 1895.

[27] Ibid., 237, 18 January 1895; 254, 15 February; 332–3, 24 May; 351, 21 June 1895.

[28] Ibid., 236, 18 January 1895. *Manchester Guardian*, 5 January 1895, 9ii; 22 January, 12iv. *Manchester City News*, 12 January 1895, 5i; 19 January, 5v.

use the Canal and left Manchester for Karachi on 28 March.[29] The Hall Line proved reluctant to use the Canal and yielded only to 'very strong representations' made by Marshall Stevens to the Bombay Conference, the *Kirby Hall* sailing from Manchester on 7 November.[30] Both the Anchor and the Clan lines maintained their regular use of the new route, while the City and Hall lines preferred to have their cargo barged to Birkenhead, paying the same toll to the Canal Company as if the goods had been loaded into steamers at Manchester.

The arrival of the Indian steamers created the greatest boom in exports in the history of the Ship Canal as Manchester began to tap the largest flow of trade ever known in the history of the world. The shipments of piece-goods more than doubled the value of cotton manufactures exported and raised the status of Manchester from the fifth port for their export in 1894 to the second from 1895, when it surpassed London, Southampton and Glasgow. The port's share in the exports of cotton manufactures from the U.K. more than doubled to 11 per cent of their value and to 14.3 per cent of their volume, proportions which were exceeded only in 1910. The total tonnage of exports increased more than that of imports during 1895 and their total value more than doubled, rising to a level surpassed only in 1903. The share of exports in the total value of the port's trade rose from 58 per cent in 1894 to the all-time peak proportion of 66.8 per cent in 1895 and the port's share of U.K. exports rose to 3.91 per cent, a proportion exceeded only in 1910. The average unit value of exports rose by 32 per cent to a pre-war peak in 1895 exceeded only in 1917 during the price inflation of the Great War.

The Canal had, however, missed in 1894 as exceptional a year in the export of cotton manufactures as it had been in the import of raw cotton. Exports of piece-goods to Bombay had risen in volume by 30 per cent during 1894 but declined in 1895 by 36 per cent in the largest reduction in Indian demand experienced during the whole fifty years

[29] B.O.D., 282, 22 March 1895. *Manchester Guardian*, 26 March 1895, 12iii; 29 March, 7viii.

[30] *Manchester Guardian*, 28 October 1895, 6i; 8 November, 6vii. B.O.D., 470, 22 November 1895.

between 1848 and 1898 under the influence of the import duty restored in 1894. That contraction in demand sharply reduced the export of piece-goods via the Canal from June 1895 as native merchants in India restricted their purchases in anticipation of the modification of the import duties which was effected in 1896.[31] The conference reduced the number of sailings, as homeward shipments from Bombay also declined, and became increasingly reluctant to send the stipulated three steamers per month up to Manchester,[32] especially as the export of piece-goods from Liverpool declined in the same proportion as their export increased from Manchester. The restraining influence of the native importers nevertheless ensured that Manchester retained its new direct trade to Bombay, even after the expiry of the last contract with the conference at the close of 1915, until the world depression of 1930.[33]

The successful entry into the Bombay trade encouraged efforts to secure for the new port a share in the shipment of piece-goods to Bengal and to China. Certain Calcutta shippers formed the Manchester Shippers' Defence Association in November 1894 and sought, with the support of the Canal Company and the Calcutta Merchants' Association, to secure the loading of Calcutta steamers at Manchester. The Calcutta Conference was the oldest of all the deep-sea conferences, having been formed in 1875, and resisted that pressure in defence of both their outward and homeward freights, retaining the loyalty of the leading shippers.[34] The Calcutta Tea Conference, re-established in 1892, controlled the exports of tea to the London market and precluded the diversion of any shipments to Manchester until 1918. The arrival of a direct cargo of tea in Manchester on 26 March 1895 marked the port's first entry into the Indian produce

[31] B.O.D., 368–9, 19 July 1895; 391–2, 16 August 1895.

[32] Ibid., 436–7, 25 October 1895; 12, 20 December 1895.

[33] Manchester Association of Importers and Exporters, *Minutes*, 70, 15 December 1915; 79, 19 January 1916. A. Redford and B. W. Clapp, *Manchester Merchants and Foreign Trade, Vol. II, 1850–1939* (Manchester University Press, 1956), 282.

[34] F. E. Hyde, *Shipping Enterprise and Management, 1830–1939. Harrison's of Liverpool* (Liverpool University Press, 1967), 79–80.

trade.[35] 'There is no commercial centre in this country which has been so closely associated with the fortunes of India or which takes so deep and watchful an interest in Indian affairs as Manchester.'[36] The first Clan Line steamers from Calcutta brought, however, only small quantities of tea and cotton to Manchester[37] and failed to follow up their pioneer voyage. Most Calcutta steamers trading regularly via the Suez Canal had become very large and ran mainly as liners, carrying such large and diverse cargoes that the Port of Manchester could not possibly be expected in the first instance to deal with full cargoes. Those vessels would not change their customary ports of discharge unless they could secure full cargoes. Thus they continued to make London, as the chief market for Oriental produce, their main destination. Manchester could not hope to succeed in entering the valuable tea trade in competition with London where even Liverpool had failed. Only in 1920 did the conference steamers of the Brocklebank and Harrison lines begin to load regularly at Manchester for Calcutta and to return with tea for distribution to England north of Birmingham.

The China shippers in Manchester acted much more effectively than the Calcutta shippers, perhaps because the China Conference had emerged victorious from the *Mogul* case in 1891 as a more formidable oligopoly than ever before under the leadership of the Ocean Steam Ship Company, managed by Alfred Holt & Co. Those shippers abstained from any attempt to drive down freights and offered to pay the existing through rates from Manchester if the conference would send their steamers to load in the new port as an experiment.[38] They persisted in their request even when they were told that no steamer over 350 ft in length could negotiate the Runcorn bend on the Canal.[39] They repeated their request on 22 November

[35] B.O.D., 192, 16 November 1894; 256, 15 February 1895.

[36] *Manchester Guardian*, 27 March 1895, 5iv, 8iii–iv.

[37] B.O.D., 413, 27 September 1895; 433, 437, 25 October 1895.

[38] T.R.C., 58, 2 August 1894.

[39] The radius of the bend was increased in 1909–11 in order to ease the passage of the Australian steamers of the Federal-Houlder-Shire Line. See *Manchester Guardian*, 22 July 1911, 7ii, 8iv, vii, for the arrival on 21 July of the *Argyllshire*, with a displacement tonnage of 19,350 and an overall length of 574 ft.

The Runcorn bend, 1893 (*Leech, op. cit., i, 304*). The sharpest curve on the Canal was also the site of the deepest cutting, excavated to a depth of 66 ft. On that bend the Canal had a width of 150 ft or a quarter more than the general bottom width of 120 ft. The Runcorn bend remained the bogey of the ship owners of Liverpool until it was modified in 1909–11, in order to ease the passage of the large Australian steamers. The bridge in the background was a high-level fixed structure built by the L.N.W.R. in 1864–68, leaving a headway of 75 ft above the Mersey. It was supplemented by the transporter bridge built in 1901–05 between Runcorn and Widnes with a clearance of 84 ft 4 in. above the waterway. Its height had, however, already determined the height of the five high-level deviation bridges built across the Canal and ensured that the masts of all vessels had to clear the bridges at 70 ft above water level.

1894 and were prepared in case of a refusal to invite non-conference lines to Manchester. Holt's capitulated after the *Rosary*, chartered by Brooks & Doxey of Gorton, had loaded a full cargo of machinery intended for a new cotton mill at Wuchang, at little over half the conference rate of freight.[40] The first Holt vessels to load for China in Manchester rather than in Birkenhead were the *Titan* in January 1895 and the *Palinurus* in March.[41] The China Mutual Line, established in 1882, brought up the largest steamers known to the Canal in the *Kaisow*, with a length of 370 ft, in March 1895 and in the *Moyune*, with a length of 410 ft, in September 1895.[42] Those vessels proved that the Canal was perfectly navigable by large steamers. The conference preserved intact its control over freight rates at the price of reducing them by 16 per cent from May 1895 but their steamers would not carry a full load of piece-goods, ostensibly for fear of encroaching upon the share of the London shipping lines. Nor would they agree to carry machinery from Manchester at Birkenhead rates, limiting their cargo to Manchester goods. Thus they frustrated the establishment of a feeder service from Bremen to Manchester by the North German Lloyd with goods for transhipment to China and Japan.[43]

The total exports of piece-goods from Britain to China increased during 1895 in sharp contrast to the reduction in shipments to India. The China steamers became, however, much fewer in the docks of Manchester during October 1895 because they had loaded more goods than the conference rules allowed and the China lines of London were threatening to load at Manchester in competition.[44] No China boats came up to load in Manchester during November,

[40] B.O.D., 195–6, 16 November 1894; 213, 19 December 1894. *Manchester Guardian*, 11 December 1894, 5iii, 'Manchester and the Eastern Trade', F. E. Hyde and J. R. Harris, *Blue Funnel. A History of Alfred Holt and Company of Liverpool* (Liverpool University Press, 1956), 107–9.

[41] B.O.D., 254–5, 25 February 1895; 282, 22 March; 315, 26 April 1895.

[42] *Manchester Guardian*, 1 April 1895, 6i; 8 April, 8vi. B.O.D., 315, 26 April 1895; 415–16, 27 September 1895.

[43] B.O.D., 284, 22 March 1895.

[44] *Manchester Guardian*, 8 November 1895, 6vii. B.O.D., 470, 22 November 1895.

when textile exports from the port sank by 38 per cent in their absence.[45] Only one vessel instead of the two expected came up to load during December and the *Tantalus* proved to be the last China steamer loaded in the Manchester docks.[46] Holt's promised a speedy resumption of regular sailings but failed to keep that promise, securing the triumph of Birkenhead and London over Manchester and restoring freights to their former level from November 1896. The loss of China shipments reduced the export of both yarn and piece-goods from their 1895 level in 1896 and 1897 as well as the share of Manchester in the export of cotton manufactures in 1896–98. Thus the new port was excluded from the fast-expanding trade with the Far East and paid a large quasi-rent or surtax in freights to Singapore, China and Japan.[47] The China Conference regained the support of China shippers in Manchester and especially of the large firms with agencies of steamship lines at Eastern ports. It continued to carry American cotton goods at lower freights than English calico and ended that discriminatory practice only in June 1902, when net freights to China were halved. The concession was made in response to two protest meetings of shippers by the Ocean Steam Ship Company, which had acquired a controlling interest in the China Mutual Line.[48] An attempt in 1912 to secure the resumption of sailings from Manchester by the China Conference was frustrated partly by the congestion caused in the port by the national seamen's strike.[49]

The advent of the China steamers in 1895 was followed by a vigorous effort by the East Mediterranean Shippers' Association of Manchester to secure a direct service from Manchester to the

45 B.O.D., 11, 20 December 1895.

46 Ibid., 41, 17 January 1896.

47 *Manchester Guardian*, 16 September 1897, 7vii; 12 January 1898, 6vii–viii. J. R. Galloway, 'Shipping rings and the Manchester cotton trade', *Journal of the Manchester Geographical Society*, July 1898, 241–63, reprinted (Manchester, Heywood, 1898, 36 pp.).

48 *Manchester Guardian*, 15 March 1902, 5iii–v; 17 April, 4vii–viii; 27 May 1902, 9vi.

49 Manchester Association of Importers and Exporters, *Minutes*, 166, 20 November 1912; 171–2, 18 December 1912.

Levant.[50] The Levant ship owners of Liverpool occupied, however, a very strong position and served as bankers to the shippers: they conceded a reduction in freights of over 50 per cent and so stilled the agitation. A regular service was nevertheless begun in 1895 from Manchester to the Persian Gulf by Bucknall Bros. and by Frank Strick & Co., being extended in 1902 by the West Hartlepool Steamship Co. Ltd.[51] The establishment of regular services to Bombay and to its outlier in the Persian Gulf represented a distinct achievement for the new port and for J. K. Bythell during the campaigning season of 1895. Manchester remained excluded from the export trade in piece-goods to the rest of Asia and Africa. It did not succeed in capturing as much of the export trade in cotton manufactures as it did of the import trade in raw cotton. Its shipments of textiles enjoyed the lowest coefficient of expansion of any of the main exports along the Canal and expanded in volume between 1895 and 1913 at only one-third of the rate of both non-textile exports and raw cotton imports. Its direct exports of cotton manufactures during the industry's final phase of expansion between 1894 and 1913 formed less than half the expected quantity and represented only 12 per cent of the industry's exports and 9.5 per cent of their value because of the dominance of cheap shipments to Bombay.

Textiles did, however, supply the Ship Canal with a staple trade essential to complement the bulk trades in coal and salt. Between 1894 and 1913 they provided 14 per cent of the increment in export tonnage and 58.7 per cent of the increment in export values. The controlling influence of cotton manufactures in the value of the port's exports was reflected in the depression of traffic in 1900 and in 1908 which was largely caused by a reduction in the export of textiles. The continued expansion in their export was facilitated by further reductions in freight which brought the net freight to Bombay by 1906 to a level 22 per cent below that of 1894. The beginning of direct

[50] B.O.D., 237, 18 January 1895; 254, 15 February; 281, 22 March 1895. *Manchester City News*, 12 January 1895, 4vi; 26 January, 5iv; 16 February, 5iii; 6 February 1897, 8vi; 25 August 1897, 4vii. *Manchester Guardian*, 14 December 1895, 5iii–v.

[51] B.O.D., 282, 22 March 1895; 415, 27 September 1895.

Table 8

Proportion of the total exports of cotton manufactures from the U.K. shipped from the Port of Manchester, 1894–1938

Period	*Volume* (%)	*Value* (%)
1894–1913	12·0	9·5
1914–29	14·1	11·4
1930–38	11·2	8·5

Source: Manchester Ship Canal, *Traffic Statistics, 1894–1938. Annual Statements of Trade*, 1894–1938.

services to Australia in 1904 and to the Levant in 1910 helped to raise the export of piece-goods from Manchester to their absolute maximum in 1911, two years before their national peak, while exports of yarn reached their absolute maximum from Manchester in 1922, thirty-eight years after the national peak of 1884. The port attained its peak proportionate share of the trade after the beginning of services to Calcutta in 1920 and to Cape Town in 1924, exporting in 1925 17.8 per cent of the total volume of the exports of cotton manufactures and 14 per cent of their total value. That peak was reached twelve years before the port handled its peak share of the import of raw cotton in 1937.

The export of machinery, like that of piece-goods, was virtually a new trade inaugurated in 1895 by the second staple industry of Lancashire. The products of the engineering industry were valuable as well as weighty and provided a perfect complement to the light goods of the cotton industry, which could not supply a full cargo and had to be loaded after heavy goods. They afforded a perfect cargo for a waterway devised, built and supported by engineers, four of whom served as directors of the Ship Canal Company, W. H. Bailey from 1886 to 1913, S. R. Platt from 1886 to 1902, C. J. Galloway from 1887 to 1904 and W. J. Crossley from 1886 to 1906.[52] Machinery was shipped first to the Baltic in exchange for oats and timber as well as to Spain and to Rio[53] Then Brooks & Doxey chartered a vessel in October 1894 to load a full cargo of machinery for China. The successful sailing of the *Rosary* in December 1894 compelled the China Conference to halve its rates for machinery in order to prevent other ships coming to Manchester. Other shipments nevertheless followed to China and then began to Bombay, which became the chief market during 1895.[54]

Shipments remained, however, restricted by the established practice of machine makers in quoting the same price f.o.b. at all ports, so in effect discriminating against Manchester by refusing to grant it a differential price.[55] The conference lines also proved reluctant to carry machinery as well as piece-goods at the same freight as from Birkenhead. Exports of machinery nevertheless increased in importance from the fifth amongst Manchester's exports in 1896 to the fourth in 1897, despite the injurious effects of an engineer's strike. In 1898 they rose in volume by an astonishing 67 per cent under the influence of the end of the strike and of the offer by Platt's of a rebate to the shippers of machinery from Manchester Docks. They surpassed the high level of 1898 only in 1905 and, stimulated by exports from the new Westinghouse factory, reached a peak in 1908 which was surpassed only in 1927 and accounted for 7 per cent of the total value of machinery exports from the U.K. The large firms remained loyal to the Canal route: by 1911 two-thirds of the shipments made by Dobson & Barlow of Bolton as well as by Brooks & Doxey passed through Manchester Docks.[56] Thus the industry employed the most

[52] *Manchester Guardian*, 8 September 1902, 5viii; 15 March 1904, 12vi; 13 October 1911, 7vii–8i; 24 November 1913, 11i and *Manchester City News*, 29 November 1913, 8ii–vii, for the obituaries of S. R. Platt (1845–1902), C. J. Galloway (1833–1904), W. J. Crossley (1844–1911) and W. H. Bailey (1838–1913).

[53] B.O.D., 163–4, 168, 19 October 1894.

[54] Ibid., 284, 22 March 1895; 335, 24 May 1895; 41, 17 January 1896.

[55] Ibid., 437, 25 October 1895.

[56] Manchester Association of Importers and Exporters, *Minutes*, 220, 20 September 1911; 16 June 1915, Minute No. 423.

Rock cutting near Ellesmere Port, 1891 (*Leech, op. cit., i, 280*).

modern means of transportation in order to equip the foreign competitors of Lancashire in Asia and in so doing became itself the residual heir of the cotton industry. Only in 1916 did textile machinists adopt a new scale of delivery charges differentiated according to port and thereby favouring Manchester.[57] The concession seems, however, to have been restricted to textile machinery.[58] The export of electrical equipment and of Ford cars created a boom in 1926–29, raising the volume of exports of machinery to an all-time peak in 1927. The world economic depression reduced the volume of exports

[57] Ibid., 147, 20 July 1916.

[58] Manchester Chamber of Commerce, Port of Manchester Committee, *Minutes*, 30, 16 November 1937, 'The Port of Manchester and the Engineering Industry'.

Eastham entrance locks under construction, 1890 (*Manchester Central Library, Local History Collection*). The two walls of the 80 ft lock are shown in the process of construction: to the left lies the sluice-way and to the right the site of the two smaller locks and the embankment separating the lock system from the Mersey estuary beyond. That system was the only one comprising three locks parallel with each other, respectively 600 ft × 80 ft, 300 ft × 50 ft and 150 ft × 30 ft. The third lock remained in use by the coasting trade from 1891 until it was closed in the 1960s. The lock gates were made of greenheart timber from Demerara

which was superior to steel, heavier than water and able to withstand the roughest use without changing shape: the pair of gates for the large 80 ft lock weighed 500 tons (Leech, op. cit., ii, 50). The adjacent sluices on the left had to withstand pressure from both tide and river and, in order to ensure stability, had gates only 20 ft in width instead of the 30 ft used at the other flood sluices on the Canal. The Eastham locks simply provided access to the Canal and did not raise vessels above sea level, unlike the four interior locks.

in 1933 to the lowest level since 1919 and stimulated the new Port of Manchester Committee to recommend in 1937 a reduction in toll by 40 per cent.[59] The handling of heavy machinery was improved by the use of cranes of progressively greater capacity, rising from 30 tons in 1894 to 60 tons in 1920 and to 250 tons in 1937,[60] after the appointment of Leslie Roberts as general manager. During the war of 1939–45 exports of machinery established their supremacy over exports of cotton manufactures, raising the average unit value of exports above that of imports. In the post-war boom shipments expanded further, supplying the Canal with one of its most remunerative traffics.

The decline of the Lancashire cotton industry was as unprecedented a phenomenon as its rise had been, profoundly affecting the economy of the whole region and the fortunes of the Ship Canal in particular. The traffic of the Canal was influenced much more in value than in volume because the cotton industry remained from 1894 the source of the most valuable export until 1942 and of the most valuable import until 1951. The process of decline was caused by the irremediable loss of the industry's export markets and was especially marked during the two decades of the 1920s and the 1950s. The share of the industry in the aggregate value of the Canal's trade, i.e. in both raw cotton and in cotton manufactures, sank from 53 per cent in 1898 and 36.5 per cent in 1928 to 19.7 per cent in 1938. The export of cotton manufactures via the Canal reached their post-war peak in 1950, one year before their national peak. From 1952 the share of cotton manufactures sank during the great oil boom below 10 per cent of the total value of exports and from 1955 the share of raw cotton sank below 10 per cent of the total value of imports.

The trade of the Canal in cotton manufactures was affected from 1912, twenty-six years before the traffic in raw cotton was similarly affected. The decline in the value of those exports contributed to the long decline from 1925 to 1940 in the total value of exports, reducing their importance in the traffic of the waterway and increasing that of imports. Cotton manufactures had furnished 69 per cent of the total

[59] Ibid., 25–35, 16 November 1937.

[60] The capacity of the port's most powerful crane, installed in 1937, was 120 tons for general traffic and 250 tons for lock gates.

value of exports during the first twenty years of operation but supplied less than half from 1930 and were surpassed in value from 1928 by the imports of raw cotton as well as by the exports of machinery from 1942.

The import of cotton goods increased at the expense of their export and so brought to the Canal a new staple import traffic in succession to the timber and grain trades as the world of Asia regained its historic supremacy in the commerce in textiles. The volume of the import of cotton goods exceeded that of exports from 1947, eleven years before the national balance of the cotton trade was reversed.[61] During 1958 Britain became for the first time since the eighteenth century a net importer of cotton goods, Lancashire manufacturers first sought government protection against foreign competition and the export of woollen manufactures via the Ship Canal first exceeded that of cotton manufactures. The shift from cotton to substitute textiles could not check the great transformation. From 1966 the exports of man-made fibre cloth were surpassed in both weight and value by imports.

The decline of the staple industry of Lancashire tilted the economic centre of gravity of the realm away from the north-west towards the south-east after 1917–18, when the joint share of Manchester and Liverpool in the foreign trade of the U.K. reached its peak proportion in the twentieth century. From 1922 London replaced Liverpool as the leading port of export and resumed its historic primacy. The resulting void in the traffic of the Canal led the Canal Company under Captain Bacon to buy the Barton Dock Estate in 1922 in order to foster the development of new industries as feeders of the Canal. The main focus of activity of the waterway began to shift away from the eastern terminal towards the western section, especially after the deepening completed in 1927, and crude oil replaced raw cotton from 1955 as the most valuable single import into the Port of Manchester.

[61] *Annual Statement of Trade*, 1948 (London, H.M.S.O., 1950), vol. IV – Supplement, 72, 75. The traffic statistics of the Ship Canal Company show that the tonnage of textile imports surpassed that of textile exports from 1959 rather than from 1947.

6

The industrialisation of Trafford Park

For over seven hundred years since the twelfth century the Traffords of Trafford had produced an uninterrupted line of male heirs and so ranked 'among the oldest of our landed families'.[1] Their name was a Norman form of the Saxon 'Stretford', where they maintained a secluded family seat by the triple-forded Irwell two miles to the west of Manchester. The Traffords had the high capacity for survival of the small landowner: they were reconverted to Catholicism about 1636, acquired a Saxon pedigree in 1638 and regained their estates after the Civil War. The family retained their local eminence in Barton and Stretford for a century after the rapid economic development of the Manchester region began in the 1780s, acquiring a baronetcy in 1841 and increasing their estates to 8,445 acres in 1873. The construction of the Manchester Ship Canal presented the greatest challenge ever known to the Traffords. They were more affected by the project than any other landed family because of the location of their lands. They proved its bitterest opponents and drove a very hard bargain with the Canal Company. Their cherished privacy was preserved only by the construction of a sandstone wall ten feet in

[1] J. H. Round, 'The Trafford Legend', *The Ancestor*, X, July 1904, 82. Idem, *Peerage and Pedigree* (London, Nisbet, 1910), ii, 56–77. W. S. G. Richards [W. U. S. Glanville-Richards], *The History of the De Traffords of Trafford circa A.D. 1000–1893* (Plymouth, Luke, 1895), adding on p. 1 a doubtful four precursors of Henry de Trafford, the 'fifth' lord of Trafford. H. T. Crofton, *A History of the Ancient Chapel of Stretford in Manchester Parish* (Manchester, Chetham Society, vol. 51 – New Series, 1903), iii, 95–151, 'The Traffords, their History and Succession', expressed his own reservations about the Trafford tradition of Saxon ancestry.

height and five miles in length, separating their lands from the new Canal. The estate remained a virtual water-girt island, bounded since 1759–64 by the Bridgewater Canal to the south and from 1894 by the wide bend of the Ship Canal in the bed of the Irwell to the north from Barton to Old Trafford, the site of the original Trafford Hall. The disposition of that property remained a matter of uncertainty for three and a half years from 1 February 1893, when Manchester Corporation established a special committee to consider its acquisition.[2]

The 1,183 acres covered an area thrice the size of Hyde Park, had acquired a high potential value because of the proximity of the Canal and could fulfil social as well as economic functions. In particular the estate might become 'a Greater Hyde Park for Greater Manchester'[3] and so provide an ideal public facility for a swelling population in dire need of recreational space. If the park passed into private hands it might be rapidly built upon, dedicated to manufacturing pursuits and surrounded by 'densely populated quarters of the poorer kind'.[4] Thus it would pollute the purest atmosphere in the district with the 'incense of industry' and, from its strategic position to the windward, would deepen what Ruskin had called the 'devil's darkness' beclouding Manchester. The Corporation was, however, heavily committed in other directions, especially to the Thirlmere and Ship Canal schemes, and was not prepared to pay the high price of £320,000–£350,000 asked by the vendors for a property outside the civic boundary. On 3 October 1894 the City Council therefore accepted the recommendation of its committee and decided not to purchase the estate.

Eighteen months later the estate was again offered for sale but was withdrawn after a maximum bid of £295,000,[5] so precipitating a new attempt to secure its purchase by the municipality.[6] Such a park

[2] Manchester Corporation, *Proceedings of Special Committees*, vol. 2, 193–4, 21 February 1893.

[3] *Manchester City News*, 8 April 1893, 4v.

[4] *Manchester Guardian*, 8 March 1894, 5iii.

[5] Ibid., 8 May 1896, 5iii.

[6] *Manchester City News*, 25 April 1896, 5ii–iii; 30 May 1896, 5ii–iii. *Manchester Guardian*, 19 May 1896, 6vii–7i; 23 May 1896, 7iii–vi.

might supply the city with such amenities as a public garden, a Rotten Row or Bois de Boulogne, a cycling track, a cricket pitch, tennis courts, parade grounds for troops, police and Volunteers and a site for the occasional Royal Agricultural Show.[7] The demand for purchase was supported by the very rich and the very poor, both of whom were relatively unaffected by the heavy burden of municipal rates.[8] The Corporation had to consider the interests of the ratepayers when faced with a request from a strong deputation urging purchase.[9] In vain did Sir John Harwood, the chairman of the Trafford Park Committee, appeal for help in acquiring the park to Salford, Eccles and Stretford. Sir Humphrey Francis de Trafford (1862–1929), the third baronet and twenty-fifth lord of Trafford, refused a final offer of £260,000 made by Harwood and sold his ancestral estate on 24 June for £360,000 to a company promoter.[10] Ernest Terah Hooley (1859–1947)[11] rose and fell with the cycle boom and slump of 1896–98, promoting twenty-six companies with a nominal capital of £18.6 million. He floated Trafford Park Estates Ltd on 17 August 1896, raised nine-tenths of its capital in London with the help of Baring's and resold to it the Trafford Hall estate for £900,000 in 'one of the biggest and the most profitable deals I ever did'.[12] Hooley decided to develop the property as a high-class residential area with five hundred villas laid out according to a plan drawn up by the London architect, R. W. Edis (1839–1927), who masked them by woods from a 200 acre racecourse and from an industrial fringe along the banks of the Ship Canal and the Bridge-

[7] *Manchester Guardian*, 13 May 1896, 5ii, 5vi–vii.

[8] Ibid., 27 May 1896, 5iii, 8iii–vi.

[9] Ibid., 23 June 1896, 7ii, 12iv.

[10] Ibid., 25 June 1896, 5i–ii, 5vi. *Manchester Weekly Times*, 26 June 1896, 4iv–v. *Manchester City News*, 27 June 1896, 6i–ii. The price of £304 per acre may be compared with that of £1,100 per acre paid for the land for Salford Docks and with that of £3,300 per acre paid for the land for Pomona Docks by the Ship Canal Company in 1888. J. D. Wallis, 'The Manchester Ship Canal Compensation Cases', *Transactions of the Surveyors' Institution*, Session 1897–98, vol. XXX: Part II, 46, 48, 22 November 1897.

[11] *The Times*, 13 February 1947, 2v.

[12] E. T. Hooley, *Hooley's Confessions* (London, Simpkin, 1925), 26–31. *The Hooley Book* (London, Dicks, 1904), 16–17, 112–16.

water Canal. Marshall Stevens, however, persuaded Hooley to develop the whole site as an industrial estate and was recruited by the great promoter to serve as general manager of the new company. Hooley himself remained chairman for only seven months until his resignation on 4 October 1897 so that he failed to fulfil his aim of making the park into a centre of the cycle and rubber trades.

Marshall Stevens (1852–1936)[13] devoted almost fifty years of his life to the service of the Port of Manchester and was buried in St Catherine's Church, Barton, close to both the Ship Canal and Trafford Park and hard by All Saints' Church, built by the Traffords in 1867–68. Together with J. K. Bythell and R. B. Stoker he became one of the three co-founders of the prosperity of the port as well as one of the creators of modern Manchester. He had entered his father's shipping business at Plymouth and had moved in 1877 to Merseyside to carry on business as a steamship agent at Garston, which lay outside the limits within which Liverpool could exact town dues. Stevens was more of an Elizabethan than a Victorian in his vitality, his buccaneering boldness and his largeness of vision. His talents were those best suited to the demands of an age of extending communications. A born shipper, he became an expert on carriage costs by sea and land and acquired an unrivalled understanding of transportation in all its aspects. In 1882 he became a member of the Provisional Committee for the Ship Canal and worked almost night and day for three years as Adamson's first lieutenant. He helped to secure parliamentary consent to the project by providing the necessary estimates of traffic and revenue. He was the first officer appointed by the Canal Company, being employed as Provisional Manager from 1885 and as General Manager from 1891,[14] fixing its tolls at half the rate of those charged via Liverpool. His most arduous task began with the opening of the Canal. During the next three critical years he

[13] *Manchester Faces and Places*, vol. V: 5, January 1894, 70–73. *Manchester Guardian*, 11 August 1936, 11iii. *The Times*, 13 August 1936, 12ii. G. Hamilton-Edwards, *The Stevens Family of Plymouth. A Record of their Achievements* (Plymouth, Hamilton-Edwards, 1949), 62–9, 72–3. Idem, *Twelve Men of Plymouth* (Plymouth, Hamilton-Edwards, 1951), 70–6, 89.

[14] B.O.D., 3–4, 11 August 1885; 239, 17 July 1891.

worked almost continuously with his staff to attract traffic and earned public praise from Bythell for his 'knowledge, resourcefulness and versatility'.[15] He secured for the company full control over the dock workers of the new port, devised the multi-floored sheds erected upon the quayside and secured the concession by the railway companies of the vital exceptional rates.[16] Stevens was tempted to become general manager of Trafford Park Estates by Hooley's offer of a salary of £2,500 and by the challenging prospect of creating 'a new Manchester' on the outskirts of the old city.[17] He was well aware of the influences which had prevented the Ship Canal from attracting the traffic he had forecast in 1886.[18] He was determined to develop the estate as a site for new factories and new firms without the financial and family ties to Liverpool of established industrialists and therefore with every incentive to make use of the Canal for their trade. That aim he sought to fulfil as managing director (1897–1929) and as chairman (1912–29). He bequeathed that aim to his son and successor, T. H. G. Stevens (1883–1970), who was appointed a director in 1919 and served as joint managing director (1924–29), managing director (1929–54) and chairman (1955–61).

A strong bond of complementary interest, especially in opposition to other ports and to their railway and shipping lines, existed between the Canal Company and Trafford Park Estates. Those common interests were reinforced by the influence of Sir William Henry Bailey, who was the largest shareholder on the board of the Canal Company, a director of the Prince Line and a director of Trafford Park Estates from 1897 until his death in 1913, leasing a site within the park in 1899 in addition to his engineering works in Salford. There were inevitable differences of view between a new and small semi-private company which proved slow to develop its resources as well as to generate traffic for the Canal and a large established public

[15] Manchester Ship Canal Company, *Report of the Directors*, 23 February 1897, 2, J. K. Bythell.

[16] B.O.D., 204, 12 February 1897; 458–9, 18 November 1898.

[17] Ibid., 217–18, 26 February 1897.

[18] Ibid., 316, 1 October 1886.

company created by statute and backed by the influence of the municipality. Those differences created friction on at least eight occasions between 1897 and 1928[19] but were always resolved through the magnitude of their mutual interest in the establishment of traffic-generating works.

The first aim of Stevens was to secure a rail link to the docks, especially after he had abandoned the idea of forming a shipping line in the Canadian trade[20] and had laid a tramway for three miles across the park.[21] He successfully urged the establishment of a railway connection upon the Canal Company.[22] Fifteen months after the tramway was first used he achieved a great triumph in the agreement of 1 November 1898, which was concluded by Bythell in anticipation of future traffic from a large landward expansion of the dock area and against the opposition of his own board of directors. That agreement provided for the construction of a rail link and for the levy of the very low rate of *6d* per ton for haulage and the provision of wagons.[23] Thus the Canal Company granted the same nominal rate for haulage between the docks and premises in Trafford Park as was then charged for haulage within the docks, although a longer and much more expensive carriage was involved. That invaluable concession became effective in 1905 when the railway companies agreed and linked up with the light railways in the park, so making them part of the dock railway system.[24] In effect it extended all the benefits of a dockside site throughout the whole of the park and remained unchanged until 1950, providing a large and continuing advantage to any factory no matter where established in the park. Stevens sought in vain to obtain even more favourable railway rates,[25] to secure through rates between Trafford Park, Bolton and Lancaster and so to make his company in effect the terminal railway company

[19] In 1897–98, 1900–01, 1904, 1909, 1914, 1917, 1922 and 1927.
[20] B.O.D., 202–3, 4 June 1897.
[21] E. Gray, *Trafford Park Tramways, 1897–1946* (Blandford Forum, Oakwood Press, 1964), 13.
[22] B.O.D., 246, 7 May 1897; 274, 2 July; 296, 13 August 1897.
[23] Ibid., 455, 4 November 1898.
[24] Ibid., 41, 18 February 1902; 168–70, 4 August 1905.
[25] Ibid., 186–9, 8 January 1909.

Panorama of the Manchester docks, 1925 (*The Illustrated London News, 2 May 1925, 823–7; by permission of the Illustrated London News Picture Library*). To the left lie the marshalling yards of Cornbrook, built up on the site of the first rail connection to the docks, established by the Cheshire Lines Committee in 1891. In the centre foreground are Pomona Docks Nos. 1–4. Opposite lie Ordsall, with the cotton mills of Sir Richard Haworth & Sons in the foreground, and the working-class housing of Ordsall, Weaste and Eccles to the right. Beyond the Trafford Road swing bridge of 1,800 tons lie Manchester Docks Nos. 6–9 and

for the docks in place of the Canal Company.[26] Those proposals were first made in 1910 and were renewed in 1913[27] but with equally little success. Trafford Park Estates never acquired any strategic basis from which to negotiate with the main-line railway companies, which preferred the longer haul from London or Liverpool to that from Manchester. Inevitably Stevens favoured the competitive development of motor haulage, proposing to the Canal Company in 1912 the establishment of a Motor Transhipment Depot in Trafford

[26] Ibid., 352–3, 4 February 1910; 382–3, 8 April 1910; 126–7, 28 July 1911; 196, 5 January 1912.

[27] Ibid., 420–1, 31 January 1913.

Trafford Wharf, 1,653 ft in length. Trafford Park is divided between the industrialised area on the left and the undeveloped Barton portion. The clear atmosphere of the industrial area of the park contrasts with the smoke of the marshalling yards and reflects the dominant role of the electric power supplied from two separate stations. In the distance may be seen the course of the Ship Canal from Mode Wheel to Barton just beyond the first curve, Runcorn at the head of the estuary and Eastham, with Liverpool and Birkenhead faintly visible.

Park for the interchange of traffic between the docks and their hinterland.

In order to attract firms Stevens had to provide the minimum necessary site facilities, including roads, railways, sewers, water, light and power. His original proposals for development in 1897 were most ambitious and included a canal basin in Davyhulme, a by-pass canal across the south-eastern corner of the estate, a dock branch of the Cheshire Lines Railway carried by tunnel beneath the Bridgewater Canal and a perimeter railway linking Eccles to Stretford and Chorlton and crossing the Ship Canal above Barton. That plan was modified drastically under the pressure of the lack of working capital caused by Hooley's bankruptcy[28] and necessitating a double issue of debentures in 1897 and 1899. Not only did Trafford Park Estates have to invest in overhead capital for the quasi-municipal development of its great fief but it also had to bear the high cost of the active pursuit of potential purchasers, since it could not afford the passive routine of a mere estate agent. The directors adopted a conservative land policy which resembled that of Bythell in relation to Ship Canal tolls, declining to sell land too cheaply, even at Barton, simply in order to manufacture a dividend. Sales were slow and progressive rents, beginning low and trebling during the first ten years of a lease, limited the initial revenue earned by the company. In order to raise the cash to pay the debenture interest Stevens had to persuade friends to establish two small subsidiaries for the development of the most valuable area of the park at its Manchester end, the Grain Elevator Estate Ltd (1899–1979) and the Throstle Nest Estate Co. Ltd, incorporated in 1901. By 1913 36 per cent of the area of the estate had been disposed of, largely on chief at increasing rentals.

In order to populate the estate Trafford Park Dwellings Ltd was registered in 1899 and was sold land very cheaply in an exception to general policy. That firm planned the construction of a model village but reduced its target from 3,000 to 1,000 cottages, completing 600 by 1903 and creating a village 'strikingly American in character' with numbered streets and avenues.[29] The dwellings company remained the least profitable of all the associated companies of Trafford Park Estates and paid no ordinary dividends from 1902 until 1929, being sold off in 1948. Transport across the park was supplied from 1897 by a gas tramway and from 1903 by an electric tramway which made profits from 1909–10 until 1932–33. A light railway was laid in 1901 by the West Manchester Light Railways Company (1899–1904) and extended by its successor, the Trafford Park Company, which was endowed by statute in 1904 with the full powers of a railway company for the operation of a purely traders' line and secured

[28] *Northern Finance and Trade*, 15 June 1898, 452, 'The Cycle Boom'; 27 July 1898, 549, 'Mr. Hooley's Affairs'.

[29] *Manchester City News*, 5 September 1903, 5iv, 'New Manchester III. The Making of an Industrial Suburb'.

recognition by the railway companies in 1905. The admission from 1905 of the tramcars of both Manchester and Salford Corporations into the park encouraged the concentration of development at the end nearest to Manchester and institutionalised the daily inflow and outflow of labour as the estate began to resemble Manchester in the diurnal rhythm of its activity, being first inundated and then forsaken by the alternation of a powerful and systematic human ebb and flow. Cottage-building was stimulated in the near-by townships, first in Salford and Stretford and then in Eccles, which was linked by a private bus service from 1922 to the western end of the park. The value of land was enhanced and revenue was generated in the form of rates, taxes and wages as well as profits. Stretford benefited most from the industrial development of the park and increased its population and its ratable value faster than any other district in the region.[30] The first power station in the park was built by Trafford Power & Light Supply Ltd (1899–1920), which was established as an associate of Glover's cable company, supplied electricity on even more favourable terms than those of Manchester Corporation and was eventually sold to Stretford Urban District Council.

The industries Stevens originally hoped to establish in the park included iron works, cotton mills, saw mills, flour mills, seed-crushing mills, malting houses and at Barton a dry dock and shipbuilding yard on the Ship Canal together with oil tanks, a coal tip and tar distilleries.[31] Those hopes were so modified that the final layout of the park bore only a limited resemblance to the original plan. For a decade Stevens resisted suggestions by manufacturers that Trafford Park Estates should become a building company, erecting factories and leasing them to manufacturers.[32] That policy was first modified in 1903, when a large cotton storage warehouse was erected for the

[30] J. S. McConechy, 'The Economic Value of the Ship Canal to Manchester', *Transactions of the Manchester Statistical Society*, 13 November 1912, 56–59.

[31] *Illustrated London News*, 13 March 1897, 365–6, 'The Trafford Park Estates'. *Northern Finance and Trade*, 3 November 1897, 368; 1 December 1897, 453. B.O.D., 324, 5 November 1897; 337, 3 December 1897.

[32] *Manchester City News*, 24 July 1897, 7ii.

Canal Company and returned a rental of 5.5 per cent on its cost.[33] Then the depression of 1908 compelled Stevens to erect cheap buildings as 'working hives' for lease in sections to manufacturers who did not wish to build. Those hives were buildings of general utility for manufacture or storage: they served as incubators for small firms and as testing laboratories for large firms new to the Manchester market. Their erection opened the estate to small manufacturers, enabling them to begin business for an annual rental of £80. The hives also inspired the construction in reinforced concrete from 1909 of cotton 'safes' which enjoyed the lowest insurance premiums in the world and were built under a self-denying compact with the Canal Company, which agreed to erect no more warehouses and to use its quay sheds for transit only.[34] The accelerated building up of the estate benefited resident contractors[35] and helped to attract concrete manufacturers to the park from 1912.

The slow pace of land sales and their concentration at the eastern end of the park divided the estate sharply between the industrialised eastern tip and the undeveloped west, which was devoted first to sports and to farming, including a Royal Agricultural Show in 1897, a golf club (1898–1911), a horse market in 1900, stockyards in 1901 and a polo ground in 1902. Manchester's first aerodrome was even established within the park in 1911 before it moved out to Barton.[36] Many negotiations proved abortive and many of Stevens's hopes were frustrated. Thus by 1912 the park had failed to attract a range of trades including shipbuilding, locomotive engineering, zinc smelting, sugar refining, seed-crushing and the manufacture of small arms, cement, creosote, chemicals, soap, paper and matches. The Manchester Patent Fuel Works Ltd (1897–1909) at Barton failed to develop a viable market in return cargoes of briquette coal for vessels using the Canal. Nor was the tea trade attracted to the park until 1918, despite the presence of Sir Joseph Lyons for twenty years

33 B.O.D., 93–4, 4 July 1902; 246–7, 1 May 1903.

34 Ibid., 291–3, 7 June 1912; 312–14, 5 July 1912; 192, 27 March 1914.

35 *The Times*, 13 October 1923, 14vi, and *Burke's Peerage* (1970, 105th edn.), 2011, for Sir Edmund Nuttall (1870–1923), civil engineer.

36 *Manchester Guardian*, 8 July 1911, 7ii–v, 12iii, 15 July, 6v; 26 July, 8ii.

(1897–1917) on the board of directors.[37]

Trafford Park represented in embryo another Manchester which grew up on a carefully planned basis alongside the old Cottonopolis. No cotton mills, no cotton spinners and no cotton manufacturers began operations in the park, whose development diversified the industrial structure of the city and reduced the relative importance therein of the cotton industry. The firms that acquired sites on the new estate were dedicated to medium and heavy industry rather than to light industry. Mostly they were limited companies, employing the most modern technology, capital-intensive methods of production and skilled labour. Being oriented to the service of the world market, they were concerned to reduce their transport costs to the minimum. Often they were international in the scope of their operations, especially after a large influx of American firms took place in 1909–13.[38] The number of those firms increased from 100 in 1915 to a peak of over 200 in 1933. Their operations made the park into Britain's most concentrated seat of capital-intensive industry.

The first firms drawn to the estate were contractors, carriers, warehousing firms and timber merchants, who established depots for storage and distribution. The milling trade was the object of Stevens's most serious efforts from 1897[39] but proved difficult to attract. A provender mill was established in 1900–01 but the first flour mills were not established until 1903–06 by the C.W.S. and by the Hovis Bread Flour Company, registered in 1898.[40] Stevens failed

37 *Northern Finance and Trade*, 2 February 1898, 82; 20 April 1898, 305, on the Lee-Enfield rifle developed in 1895; B.O.D., 313–15, 25 September 1903, on Manchester Oil-Seed Crushers Ltd; ibid., 109, 31 March 1905, and 20, 6 September 1907, on the Darwen Paper Mill Co. and the Thames Paper Co. See *The Times*, 23 June 1917, 9iii, for the obituary of Lyons.

38 The Rubber Regenerating Co. Ltd and the English Grains Co. Ltd in 1909, the Southern Cotton Oil Co. Ltd of Great Britain, the English Textilose Manufacturing Co. and the Ford Motor Co. Ltd in 1911, the British Reinforced Concrete Engineering Co., the Dominion Register Co. of Canada and the Carborundum Co. of Niagara in 1912, the Trussed Concrete Steel Co. and the Xylos Rubber Co. in 1913.

39 B.O.D., 284–6, 16 July 1897.

40 Ibid., 316–18, 25 September 1903; 441–6, 3 June 1904; 32–4, 18 November 1904.

in 1911 to secure a government subsidy for the establishment of another grain elevator as part of a grand design to accumulate a war-time reserve supply of grain for the nation. Most characteristic of the park became the archetypes of modern industry in the oil trade, engineering and, from 1912, the chemical industry. The oil industry was first established at Mode Wheel in 1897 and was then planted at the Barton end of the park in 1899, attracting investment by American oil companies from 1902. Engineering works, especially for the new industry of electrical engineering, were drawn to the estate from 1898 onwards, especially under the influence of Sir William Bailey.

In 1899 the British Westinghouse Electric Company was floated under the auspices of Rothschild's as a British subsidiary of the American firm of George Westinghouse. The new company bought 130 acres, or 11 per cent, of the entire estate, establishing itself on the clay lands in the south-eastern corner until then leased by the Trafford Brick Co. Ltd (1897–1900). It erected at high speed the largest engineering works in the kingdom, in anticipation of a rapid electrification of British railways on the American pattern. A vast machine shop was modelled on American lines and equipped with gigantic machine tools at a total cost of £1.7 million, representing 69 per cent of the capital of £2.45 million invested in local engineering during the four years 1899–1902.[41] The firm introduced trans-atlantic techniques of building, manufacture and industrial training, employing American foremen and retraining English engineers at Pittsburgh. The American founder exported the name of the estate to Pennsylvania, where he established Trafford City in 1902 fourteen miles to the east of Pittsburgh. British Westinghouse began the manufacture in 1902 of steam turbines and of turbo-generators, securing contracts for the electrification of railways in Liverpool and London. Occupying the largest single site in 'Traffordville',[42] the firm immediately became and remained the largest employer in the park. With 6,000 hands in 1903, it raised the total number employed

[41] *Proceedings of the Manchester Association of Engineers*, 17 January 1903, 9, E. G. Constantine, 'Inaugural Address'.

[42] J. Dummelow, *1899–1949* (Manchester, Metropolitan-Vickers Electrical Co. Ltd, 1949), 7.

on the estate sharply from 5,000 on 30 June 1902 to 12,000 by 28 October 1903.[43] In order to help float the bonds of client companies it established its own finance company in the Traction & Power Securities Co. Ltd, which was registered in 1901 and was successively renamed the Traction and General Investment Trust Ltd in 1927 and the British American and General Trust Ltd in 1957. Westinghouse had, however, begun production at the end of the boom of 1896–1903 in the electrical industry and had overestimated the absorptive capacity of the market. The company suffered from the failure of British railways to adopt electrification, from the lack of any large demand for electric motors in the textile industry and from the competition of the gas industry as well as of the steam engine. Its quest for orders at almost any price ushered in an era of price-cutting which reduced Ferranti's of Hollinwood to bankruptcy in 1903. Its competition stimulated local engineers to form a new Engineering Section in the Manchester Chamber of Commerce in 1901 and its demands attracted other firms in the iron and steel trades to Trafford Park. As a school of technology the firm remained unrivalled:[44] as a commercial enterprise it proved remunerative only to the debenture holders and paid no dividend to its ordinary shareholders until 1919, after its reorganisation as Metropolitan Vickers Electrical Co. Ltd. Only the demands of war raised its employment of labour to the peak level of 30,000 in 1943–44. Nevertheless it reduced British dependence upon imports after 1902[45] and it began the introduction of American firms to the park, a process carried further in 1909–13 and in 1926–31. Not only did the company establish Manchester's first radio station, in 1922, but it also provided the Ship Canal with a trade of growing value in the import of copper, surpassed only by silver in electrical conductivity.

[43] *Manchester City News*, 5 September 1903, 5iv.

[44] *Engineering*, 14 July 1899, 51–2; 28 March 1902, 397–8; 20 January 1928, 64–8—29 June 1928, 815–17, nine articles reprinted as *The Trafford Park Works of the Metropolitan-Vickers Electrical Co. Ltd., Manchester* (Manchester, 1929, 176 pp.).

[45] I. C. R. Byatt, *The British Electrical Industry 1875–1914* (Oxford, Clarendon Press, 1979), 167.

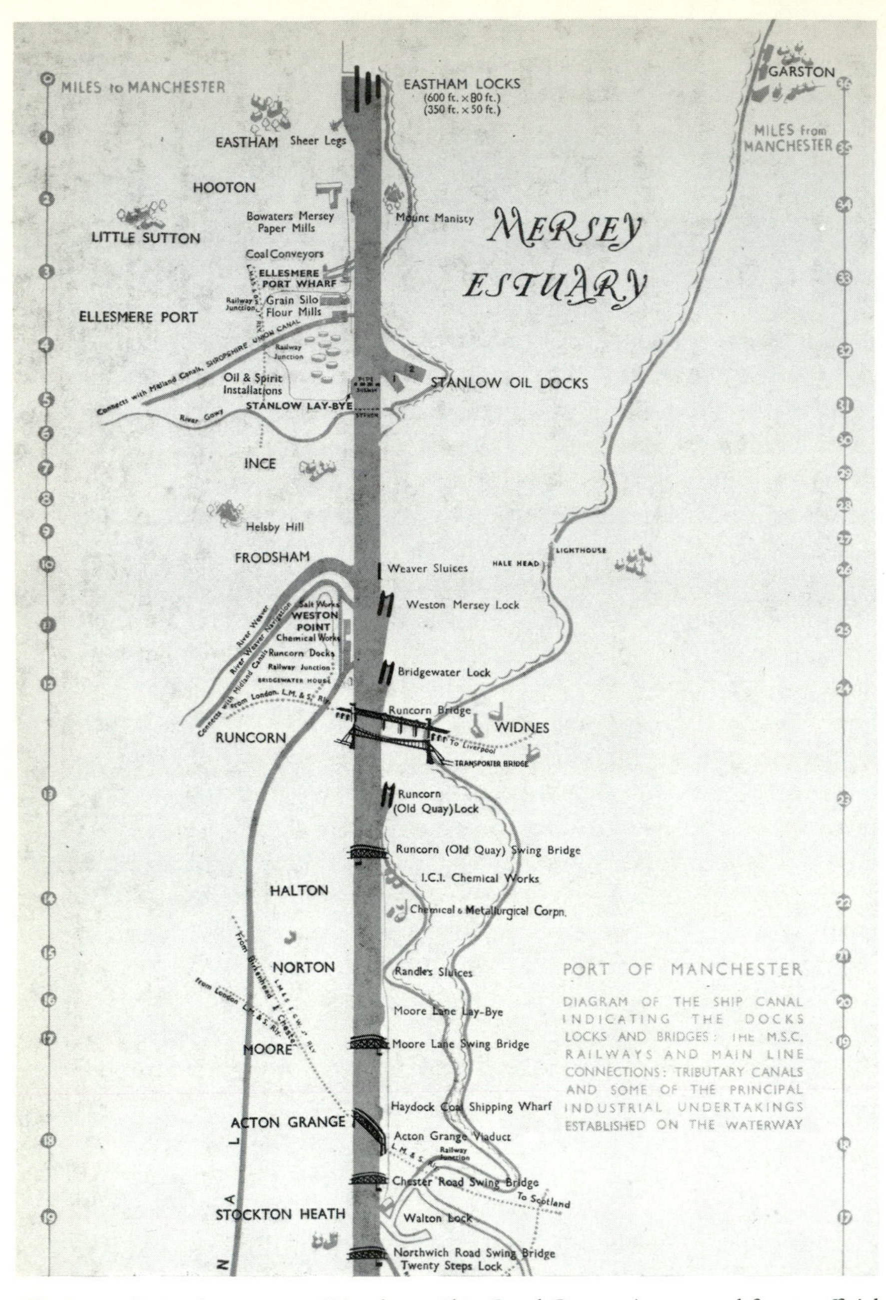

The Port of Manchester, 1935 (*Manchester Ship Canal Company*); prepared for an official visit by the members of the Manchester Chamber of Commerce on 4 July 1935 before the inauguration of the Port of Manchester Committee.

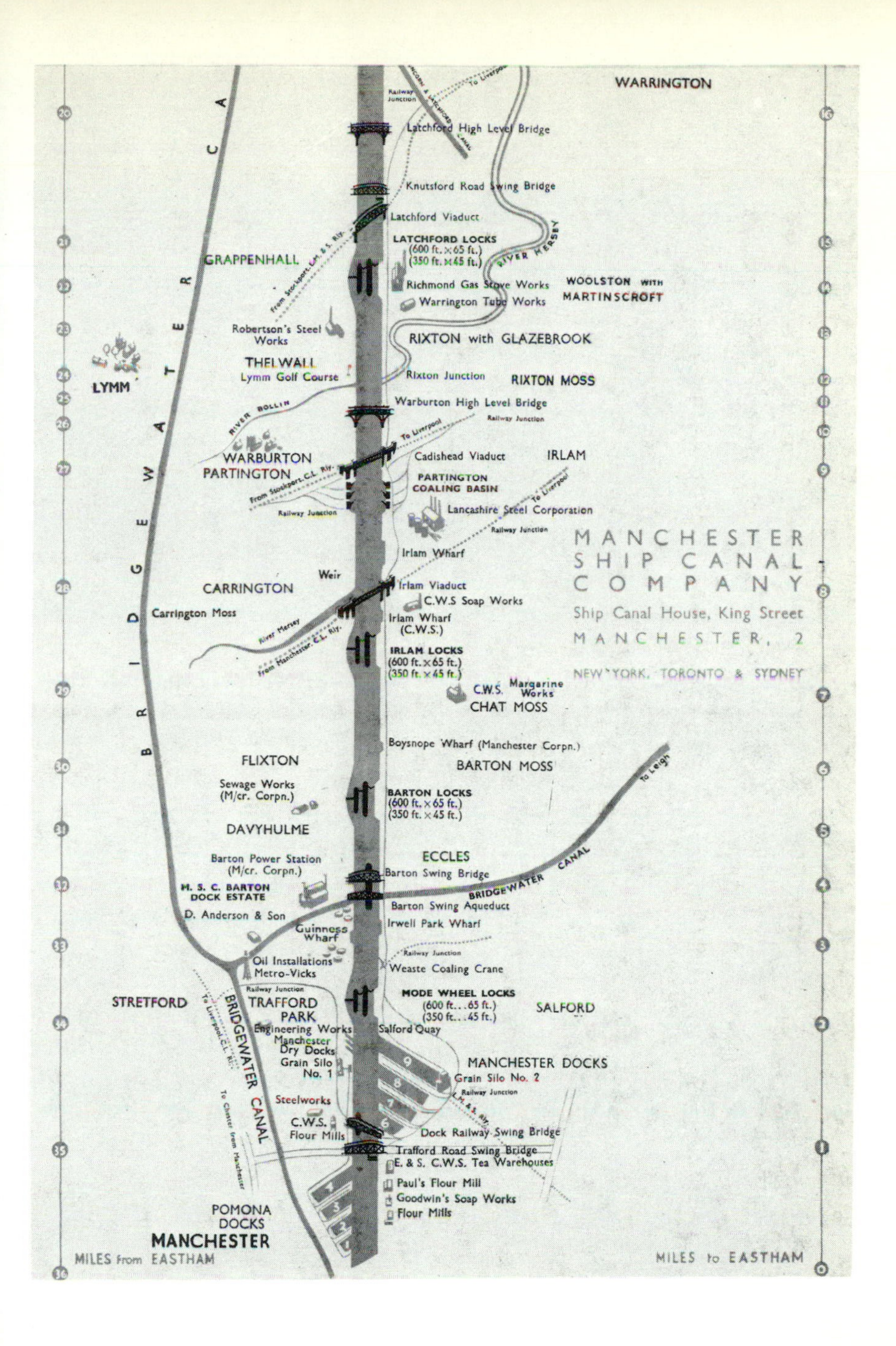

WARRINGTON
Latchford High Level Bridge
Knutsford Road Swing Bridge
Latchford Viaduct
LATCHFORD LOCKS
(600 ft. × 65 ft.)
(350 ft. × 45 ft.)
RIVER MERSEY
GRAPPENHALL
Richmond Gas Stove Works
Warrington Tube Works
WOOLSTON WITH MARTINSCROFT
Robertson's Steel Works
RIXTON with GLAZEBROOK
THELWALL
Lymm Golf Course
Rixton Junction
RIXTON MOSS
LYMM
Warburton High Level Bridge
Railway Junction
RIVER BOLLIN
To Liverpool
Cadishead Viaduct
IRLAM
WARBURTON
PARTINGTON
PARTINGTON COALING BASIN
From Stockport. C.L. Rly.
Railway Junction
Lancashire Steel Corporation
MANCHESTER SHIP CANAL COMPANY
Ship Canal House, King Street
MANCHESTER, 2
NEW YORK, TORONTO & SYDNEY
Irlam Wharf
Weir
CARRINGTON
Irlam Viaduct
C.W.S Soap Works
Carrington Moss
Irlam Wharf (C.W.S.)
River Mersey
From Manchester. C.L. Rly.
IRLAM LOCKS
(600 ft. × 65 ft.)
(350 ft. × 45 ft.)
C.W.S. Margarine Works
CHAT MOSS
BRIDGEWATER CANAL
Boysnope Wharf (Manchester Corpn.)
FLIXTON
BARTON MOSS
Sewage Works (M/cr. Corpn.)
BARTON LOCKS
(600 ft. × 65 ft.)
(350 ft. × 45 ft.)
To Leigh
DAVYHULME
ECCLES
Barton Power Station (M/cr. Corpn.)
Barton Swing Bridge
M. S. C. BARTON DOCK ESTATE
Barton Swing Aqueduct
D. Anderson & Son
Irwell Park Wharf
Guinness Wharf
Railway Junction
Oil Installations
Metro-Vicks
Weaste Coaling Crane
Railway Junction
MODE WHEEL LOCKS
(600 ft. . . 65 ft.)
(350 ft. . . 45 ft.)
STRETFORD
TRAFFORD PARK
SALFORD
To Liverpool C.L. Rly.
Engineering Works
Salford Quay
Manchester Dry Docks
Grain Silo No. 1
MANCHESTER DOCKS
Grain Silo No. 2
Railway Junction
Steelworks
To Chester from Manchester
C.W.S. Flour Mills
Dock Railway Swing Bridge
Trafford Road Swing Bridge
E. & S. C.W.S. Tea Warehouses
Paul's Flour Mill
Goodwin's Soap Works
Flour Mills
POMONA DOCKS
MANCHESTER
MILES from EASTHAM
MILES to EASTHAM

Marshall Stevens sought to enhance the value of the park's one-and-a-half mile frontage upon the Ship Canal and to overcome its lack of docks and wharves. Despite repeated efforts he failed to interest either the Canal Company or any railway company in the acquisition of that valuable site for docks and he did not dispose of any land fronting upon the Canal until 1911. In a prospectus and plan of the estate in 1898 he claimed the right to berth vessels in the fairway of the Canal on the Trafford Park side in contravention of the rights of the Canal Company.[46] Then in a dramatic coup on 7 November 1899 he purchased the racecourse from the Manchester Racecourse Co. Ltd for £280,000,[47] so anticipating the Canal Company's need for land for its projected new dock, extending the influence of Trafford Park Estates across the Canal on to the Salford bank and claiming the right to undertake the construction of a new dock of fifty to sixty acres as well as to provide for another dock south-west of Trafford Wharf. Stevens hoped to achieve a large extension of the function of his company at the expense of the Canal Company, to become a public dock company, to supply the future requirements of trade as well as its immediate needs and to earn a dividend of 23 per cent.[48] J. K. Bythell and Alderman Southern concluded that Stevens wished to acquire all the land to the north as well as to the south of the docks, to hem them in on both sides and so to try 'to throttle the Ship Canal in the future'.[49] In fact Stevens did propose that the dock terminal should be separated from the Canal and transferred as an unremunerative enterprise to the Corporation, that the Canal Company should be restricted in function to the receipt of Canal tolls and that the future development of the terminal should be entrusted to other bodies, either corporations, landowners or terminal companies.[50] The purchase of the racecourse

46 B.O.D., 441–2, 7 October 1898.

47 Ibid., 117, 3 November 1899; 122–6, 17 November 1899.

48 Ibid., 322–6, 14 December 1900.

49 Manchester Ship Canal Company, *Report of the Directors*, 21 February 1900, 12, J. K. Bythell and J. W. Southern.

50 Ibid., 8 August 1901, 12, M. Stevens.

provoked an immediate response from the Canal Company,[51] which secured a legal injunction upsetting the sale and considered cutting off rail traffic to Trafford Park.[52] Trafford Park Estates at first offered to sell the racecourse to the Canal Company for £1 million[53] but was then forced to resort to arbitration and to accept an award of £262,500, or £2,645 per acre, with £22,764 in costs. The award safeguarded the fundamental interests of Trafford Park Estates by preventing any depreciation in land values and by preventing the Canal Company from competing with it by the sale of dockside sites for industrial development.

Undaunted by his setback, Stevens tried during the boom of 1902 in American cotton and shipping to attract a syndicate from the U.S.A. to construct a railway dock terminal on an eighty-acre site on the undeveloped Canal frontage north of Trafford Hall. He then proposed in the Trafford Park Dock and Railway Bill of 1904 to construct an ocean and railway terminal in the park to be worked as a public dock estate with all the special rights and privileges of the Canal Company.[54] That project failed to secure the support of any railway in the U.S.A. and aroused the determined and successful opposition of the Manchester Corporation and the Canal Company. In self-defence the Canal Company refused to sanction in 1913 a project to construct wharves on the Ship Canal at Barton[55] and in 1914 a request to build a bridge over the Bridgewater Canal at Barton to the Barton Dock Estate which lay beyond.[56] Thus it imposed limits upon a new project of expansion by Trafford Park Estates, which penned a bitter letter of complaint to the board of directors.[57] Stevens did, however, extend the functions of his com-

[51] B.O.D., 143, 15 December 1899; 156, 19 January 1900; 222–3, 1 June; 227–8, 15 June 1900.

[52] Ibid., 237–40, 29 June 1900.

[53] Ibid., 334–5, 28 December 1900.

[54] Ibid., 375, 31 December 1903; 379–80, 5 January 1904; 418–19, 25 March 1904.

[55] Ibid., 420–1, 31 January 1913; 93, 24 October 1913; 172–3, 20 February 1914; 292, 6 November 1914.

[56] Ibid., 161, 13 February 1914.

[57] Ibid., 370–5, 26 March 1915.

pany into the profitable field of warehousing, which it had entered in 1902–03 and had developed from 1911–12 by erecting fireproof cotton storage 'safes' for the Canal Company. In 1914 he formed an associate company in the Port of Manchester Warehouses Ltd, which took over the operation of the cotton 'safes' and benefited by the great wartime demand for storage space: it adopted mechanical handling devices and proved to be the most successful of all the sub-subsidiary trading companies of Trafford Park Estates.[58] At the close of the war Stevens was drawn in 1917 into a tripartite duel with the railway companies and the Canal Company over the issue of accommodation and rates for rail traffic. Therein he sought to expand into the spheres of banking and haulage and to secure the transfer of the functions of warehousing and carting from the railways to private hands.[59] The Port of Manchester Road Service Ltd (1921–30) was created as a haulage subsidiary and used steam lorries and insulated vans for the rapid distribution of goods within a thirty-mile radius of the docks where the railways could not compete. It failed, however, to survive the fierce competition of private hauliers.

The pace of development of the estate proved too slow for the Manchester shareholders, who held one-tenth of the capital of Trafford Park Estates and provided abundant stimulating criticism of the policies of the management. For the first ten years of its life the company spent more than it earned and for the first twelve it worked in effect for the debenture holders. The directors renounced in succession their commission on sales in 1904 and part of their fees in 1911. The company first made a profit in 1905–06 and first paid an ordinary dividend in 1908–09, so entering upon a career of uninterrupted dividends. Only in 1913–14 did it pay a dividend wholly out of revenue and only from 1914–15 did it return a reasonable dividend of 4 per cent.

The war of 1914–18 brought the port and the park into full use,

[58] Port of Manchester Warehouses Ltd, *Then and Now* (Manchester, Port of Manchester Warehouses, 1921, 48 pp., illustrated by W. Heath Robinson).

[59] Manchester Association of Importers and Exporters, *Minutes*, 31, 9 March 1917; 268, 11 July 1918. A. Redford and B. W. Clapp, *Manchester Merchants and Foreign Trade, Vol. II, 1850–1939* (1956), 207–8.

especially for the manufacture of munitions, chemicals and aircraft. Under the pressure of wartime demand much more of the estate was occupied, sharply reducing the vacant proportion from 51 per cent in 1915 to 34 per cent in 1921. In the post-war boom Marshall Stevens secured election as Unionist M.P. for Eccles (1918–22), advocating commercial policies similar to those of R. B. Stoker, and the revenue earned by Trafford Park Estates reached an all-time maximum in the boom year of 1920–21, returning 9 per cent gross upon its capital. The company had increased the number of its Manchester directors in 1911 from two out of six to three out of six: in 1921 it elected to the board the first representative of the traders of Trafford Park in the head of Taylor Bros., which had begun in 1909 to manufacture steel forgings for railway companies and had pioneered the development of the south-western part of the park in Davyhulme. George R. T. Taylor (1876–1965) served as a director from 1921 until 1949 and as chairman of the company from 1943 to 1949. The company also enlarged its capital with the aid of loans from 1923 to a peak in 1927 and embarked upon a new phase of expansion, extending its railway sidings to their maximum length and founding a new clutch of subsidiaries.

Trafford Park Cold Storage Co. Ltd was incorporated in 1918 and provided more cubic capacity than either the Corporation or the Union Cold Storage Co. Ltd: its stores were built for the beef and mutton of Australia but had to accept small consignments of eggs and fruit and only became a permanent success from 1928–29. Manchester Consignments Ltd (1922–29) was founded with the aid of loan capital to encourage the import of produce from Australia and New Zealand via the Ship Canal. Brooke Bond & Co. Ltd established a large warehouse in 1922 for the blending and packing of tea, diverting a large tonnage away from the London tea ring and stimulating emulation by the C.W.S. in 1929. The Trafford Park Bacon Factory Ltd (1923–28) failed, however, to emulate the success of the C.W.S. in another field: it could not establish a local market for bacon made by a Toronto packer from Canadian hogs and sold in competition with Danish bacon.[60] The Ford Motor Co. Ltd had begun operations

60 *Manchester City News*, 10 October 1925, 13iii, 'Manchester's Imports'.

on a ten-acre site in the park in 1910, undertaking the assembly of the cheapest cars on the British market. From Detroit the firm imported first cars and then parts, taking over Trafford Park Woodworkers Ltd in 1913 in order to secure a supply of bodies and to save on freights.[61] The popularity of the Model T enabled Ford's to become the largest car manufacturer in the country by 1913. The firm reached the peak of its production in the post-war boom of 1920, when it first became subject to discriminatory taxation on the horse-power of its engines. Thereafter it lost ground to Morris and Austin, especially after 1926, and was driven into the export market. In order to exploit the European market Ford's moved in 1931 with 2,000 skilled workers to rural Dagenham, where it had acquired 300 acres in 1928 for the establishment of an enormous new works, enjoying easy access from its own dock on the Thames to its intended mart across the Channel.

The international depression of 1929–32 compelled Trafford Park Estates to reduce its capital and its commitments, winding up its three subsidiaries, for bacon in 1928, for consignments in 1929 and for road transport in 1930. It did not, however, plunge the park's traders into bankruptcy, affecting them much less than other firms within the Manchester region. The war of 1939–45 transformed the estate into the greatest arsenal of war production in the kingdom, raising employment by 50 per cent to a peak level of 75,000 and attracting heavy German air raids on 22–23 December 1940 which destroyed Trafford Hall and wreaked havoc throughout the park and docks. A heavy fiscal price was paid for victory as taxation increased its share of the company's profits fivefold from 12 per cent in 1938–39 to 61 per cent in 1951–52. After the war the park reached maturity as the proportion of land unleased declined from 15 per cent in 1945 to 8 per cent in 1958. Trafford Park Estates had successfully transformed a deer park of 1.9 square miles into the first and largest industrial estate in Europe, without the benefit of subsidy or aid from any authority, central or local. That power-house of industry generated traffic for the Ship

[61] *Manchester Guardian*, 14 November 1911, 15ii.

Canal and became even more important than Manchester Liners as an indirect source of revenue to the Canal Company.

In 1964–65 Trafford Park began to pay the price of the pioneer as it faced competition from trading estates sponsored by the government as well as by the Canal Company. The 1,000 acre Barton Dock Estate had been bought by the Canal Company in 1921 from the Trustees of the De Trafford Estates but was developed only during the war and effectively prohibited further expansion to the south across the Bridgewater Canal. The tonnage of goods carried on the estate railways declined from their peak of 1941 and were burdened by increased railway rates after the revocation in 1950 of the 'charter' of 1898. The great oil boom at Stanlow in the 1950s set in motion the industrial development of the western section of the Ship Canal, which inherited the dynamic role assumed by Trafford Park in the 1900s. In the decade of the 1960s the park began to adapt to the challenge of the motorway, becoming in 1967–70 the centre of a motorway and rail Freightliner network, losing its main-line rail service in 1969 and abandoning its marshalling sidings in 1972. The decline of employment within the park from 75,000 in 1945 and 60,000 in 1967 to 15,000 in 1976[62] threatened the economic base of the new metropolitan borough of Trafford which was created in 1974 from the three boroughs of Stretford, Sale and Altrincham and extended its limits to the Ship Canal on the north and as far west as the river Bollin. In order to respond to that challenge the Trafford Park Industrial Council was established in 1971.

Under the guiding hand of Baring Bros. Trafford Park Estates converted itself from 1958 into a holding company. It trebled its capital in 1962–64 in order to enable its shares to qualify as trustee investments. It transformed its associate companies into wholly owned subsidiaries and sold off the cold storage business in 1972. The process of development had reduced its direct interest in Trafford Park and had even created competitive mini-industrial estates within the original confines of its vast fief but stimulated it to enter upon a

[62] *Manchester Evening News*, 25 October 1967, 9vi. *Financial Times*, 22 April 1971, 32vi; 12 March 1976, 33i.

new phase of its career. The company began to acquire land in developing parts of the U.K., especially on industrial estates, at Hereford in 1964, at Wakefield and Sunderland in 1967 and at Hooton as well as Wigan in 1973. For the administration of its new properties it began to establish a new clutch of subsidiaries, including Trafford Industrial Buildings Ltd in 1964, Trafford Extensions Ltd in 1965 for its office premises at Baguley, and Calder Vale Estates Ltd in 1968 for its holding at Wakefield. The profits of its trading subsidiaries became more important and the share of rents in its income, 92.6 per cent in 1907–08 and 88.2 per cent in 1949–50, sank to 39 per cent in 1965–66. Dividends declined from their peak level of 1962 but averaged a respectable 8 per cent over the eighty-two years 1896–1978. Thus the park provided the launching pad for a modern property firm as well as for a family trust. The Trustees of the De Trafford Estates had been established in 1855 and vested in 1904 with full powers of management of the family's extensive properties in Lancashire and Cheshire. The original cradle and seat of the Traffords remained, however, a seed-bed of modern technology and a quietly humming mass of capital-intensive industry, largely unaffected by strikes or the threat of strikes. It formed a living memorial to a dynamic businessman, who was also commemorated in a 22 ton block of grey granite erected in the heart of the park in 1937.[63]

[63] *Manchester Guardian*, 7 September 1937, 13v; 1 October, 13v, 14iii–iv.

7

The great oil boom, 1922–75

The traffic of the Ship Canal was dominated in succession by the two great tides of modern world commerce, the export of cotton textiles in the nineteenth century and the import of petroleum in the twentieth century. Created to serve the needs of the dominant trade of Lancashire, the Canal successfully adapted itself to the decline of the cotton industry and to the supersession of cotton goods by oil as the object of the largest trade in the world. That process of adaptation was a necessary but passive response to the development of America and reflected the shift of economic supremacy from Britain to the U.S.A. The oil trade was controlled not by Britain but by the U.S.A. and by a few large firms managing a highly capitalised industry and catering for an international market. Those firms supplied a demand for fuel which increased faster, especially in Lancashire, than that for any other commodity. 'Manchester is probably the centre of the most important oil-consuming district in the world.'[1] Thus imports of oil via the Canal consistently expanded more rapidly than those of any other main import, more than fulfilling the expectations of the promoters of the waterway.

During the first seven years of the Canal's operation oil imports increased in each successive year, whereas timber imports enjoyed only four years of continuous expansion from 1894, cotton imports five such years and grain imports six. Between 1894 and 1913 those imports increased on average twice as fast as all non-oil imports together, between 1894 and 1959 they increased more than three

[1] *Manchester Guardian*, 7 June 1898, 5vi.

times as fast and during the boom years between 1946 and 1959 they increased more than five times as fast. The history of the oil trade of the Canal falls into four main phases, each of which was largely identified with a single product. The import trade was dominated in succession by lamp oil from 1895 to 1924, by petrol from 1925 to 1949 and by crude oil from 1950 to 1962. Imports declined from their peak tonnage of 1959, while exports of refined products increased, especially from 1963, to usher in a new chapter in the history of the Canal.

Oil provided one of the more profitable traffics of the waterway, since it paid the same rewarding toll as timber or grain. Unlike raw cotton, it was, however, more important in the volume than in the value of its traffic. Indeed, petroleum lent itself to bulk transport by specialised tank ship, to unloading by pipes without intermediate handling by dockers and to storage in large tanks pending distribution. Tankers could not, however, use the Canal until tanks had been built to receive their cargo and such tanks could only be safely established in complete isolation from the docks proper. The establishment of such facilities at a distance from the Canal terminal would have introduced a new trade into the Manchester district but failed to attract either local or metropolitan investors. Marshall Stevens had begun to pursue the bulk oil trade in 1893 and continued his efforts without success for almost three years after the opening of the Canal. Less capital was needed to establish oil tanks than other essential canalside facilities but the necessary funds could not be secured either from the large oil companies or from any of their potential competitors. The first attempt to establish a local oil storage company failed to raise the necessary capital for such a risky venture.[2] Both the Russian and the American oil companies declined to erect oil tanks and to use Manchester as a centre for distribution.[3] Thus the import of oil remained a cask trade from 1894 until 1897. It began with the shipment of lubricating oil from Philadelphia and New York[4] and was then extended to the import of the cheaper 'petroleum oil' or lamp

2 B.O.D., 252, 1 February 1895; 306–7, 314, 26 April 1895.
3 Ibid., 332, 24 May 1895; 350, 21 June 1895.
4 *Manchester Guardian*, 7 May 1894, 8v; 9 August 1894, 8iii.

oil,[5] so reducing the average unit price of oil imports during the next eight years. Standard Oil arranged with Lamport & Holt in August 1895 for the regular shipment of lamp oil from New York direct to Manchester for distribution by its English subsidiary, the Anglo-American Oil Company, which had been founded in 1888 and had become the country's largest importer of paraffin. The establishment of the trade upon a firm footing encouraged the erection of tanks by a number of small proprietors.

The first agreement with the Canal Company for the erection of such tanks at Mode Wheel to receive the shipments made by Standard Oil was concluded on 25 January 1896 by Bagnall & Co., which had begun business in 1866.[6] Then the board of directors of the Canal Company approved on 16 July 1897 strict safety regulations for tank oil steamers carrying oil with a safe flashpoint above 73°F.[7] On 24 July the first tanker began to unload 3,600 tons from Philadelphia at the new oil gas depot of Manchester Corporation at Mode Wheel, next to the Foreign Animals Wharf, enabling the municipality to experiment in the use of oil for the manufacture of gas.[8] The first oil tanker from Batum arrived in September 1897 and so opened up a larger source of supply.[9] The admission of tankers to the Canal raised the volume of bulk oil imports above that of cask oil from 1897 and helped to increase the tonnage of oil imports almost eightfold during 1897 and 1898. Storage capacity was built up outside the docks at Mode Wheel from 1896, at Eccles close to Irwell Park from 1897, at the Barton end of Trafford Park from 1901 and at Weaste from 1904.[10] The completion of the first four installations by January 1898 ushered in a new era in the history of Mode Wheel.[11]

[5] B.O.D., 412, 27 September 1895; 432, 25 October 1895.

[6] Ibid., 140, 25 September 1896; 287–8, 16 July 1897; 375, 11 March 1898; 3, 27 January 1899. W. G. Bagnall, *Seventy Years of my Life* (Rochester, Stanhope, 1937), 22–38, 'Petroleum and the Nations'.

[7] B.O.D., 288–9, 16 July 1897; 154, 19 January 1900.

[8] *Manchester Guardian*, 24 July 1897, 7v; 31 July 1897, 5v.

[9] Ibid., 4 September 1897, 8vii; 8 December 1897, 4vi.

[10] B.O.D., 433–4, 20 September 1901; 464–8, 29 July 1904.

[11] *Manchester Courier*, 15 February 1898, 10v, 'The Ship Canal and the Bulk Oil Trade'.

The construction of an oil berth on the Ship Canal at Barton in 1902 dedicated another locality to the service of the oil industry. Exports of oil were recorded first in 1904 but never became as important as imports.

Bulk imports flowed to Manchester from the Black Sea rather than from America as Russia became the largest oil producer in the world between 1898 and 1901. Manchester rose rapidly from the position of the seventh largest importer of oil in 1896 to that of the fifth in 1897, the third in 1898 and the second after London in 1899. It first surpassed Liverpool as the second oil port of the kingdom in the quantity of its oil imports in 1899 and in the value thereof in 1907 but left unchallenged the vast import trade in palm oil from West Africa to the Mersey. Amongst the direct imports into Manchester oil ranked sixth in tonnage from 1898 and third from 1907. From 1911 it supplied the third most valuable import into the port after cotton and grain. The traffic in oil became relatively more important than that in either grain or timber because it catered for a larger hinterland, using canal barges and rail tank cars to supply the West Riding and the Midlands. During the first twenty years of operation from 1894 to 1913 the Port of Manchester imported 10.2 per cent of the total volume of imports of oil into the country. Manchester had established its position as a distribution centre for Russian oil and therefore aroused the interest of the giant Standard Oil Company. The U.S.A. regained its supremacy as the world's largest producer from 1902, when the Anglo-American Oil Company purchased the installation of the Bagnall Oil Co. Ltd and began to expand its operations at Mode Wheel.[12] The parent of Shell-Mex Ltd, the Producers' Petroleum Company, also established five tanks at the Barton end of Trafford Park in 1910 and expanded its import of Mexican crude from 1915[13] as Weetman Pearson (1856–1927) developed the oil resources of Mexico.

[12] B.O.D., 75, 30 May 1902.
[13] Ibid., 439, 27 August 1915.

The war of 1914–18 completed the ousting of Russian by American oil and carried the import of cask oil to its all-time maximum tonnage in 1916, so permitting the triumph of the tanker over the cargo vessel. Oil imports ceased, however, to expand and did not exceed their level of 1913 until 1921. The war nevertheless ushered in a new era in the history of the oil trade of the port because the Canal Company for the first time permitted petrol tankers to navigate the waterway in the service of the Admiralty.[14] In peacetime the directors had recognised the danger to other vessels of traffic in oil products, such as petrol, with a flashpoint below 73°F and especially the hazards involved in the use by tankers of four separate sets of locks between the sea and Mode Wheel. They had reaffirmed their decision to exclude such products four times,[15] declining to follow the example set by the Suez Canal Company in 1907.

After the war the Canal Company built at Stanlow promontory, five miles east of the Eastham lock entrance, an isolated and separate oil dock for the import of products with a dangerously low flashpoint such as petrol. The construction of that dock between 1919 and 1922 ushered in a new era in the history of the Canal by inaugurating a fundamental shift of activity from the Manchester docks to the Ellesmere Port section. The Stanlow Oil Dock, opened on 6 June 1922,[16] proved an immediate success and became a growing source of revenue to the Canal Company. The oil trade continued to expand at the Manchester terminal, especially at Barton, which attracted the Anglo-American Oil Company in 1920, Cory Bros. & Co. in 1926, the Texas Oil Company in 1928 and the Manchester Oil Refinery Ltd, which undertook from 1938 the blending and distilling of specialised industrial oils. The new Barton Power Station opened by Manchester Corporation in 1923 used, however, not oil but coal. The large-scale improvement of facilities nevertheless became concentrated for the next forty years in the Ellesmere Port section, post-

[14] Ibid., 375, 26 March 1915.

[15] Ibid., 3, 27 January 1899; 403, 18 February 1904; 117–18, 15 May 1908; 143–4, 31 July 1908; 334–5, 24 December 1909.

[16] *The Engineer*, 29 September 1922, 324–6, 'Petroleum Spirit Dock on the Manchester Ship Canal'.

Stanlow oil docks, 1929 and 1962 (*Manchester Ship Canal Company; Air Views (Manchester) Ltd, Manchester Airport*).

Oil Dock No. 1 (1922), with the tank farms planted on the marshland west of Ince beyond the Canal and linked by subterranean pipeline to the oil berths.

Oil Docks No. 1 (1922) and No. 2 (1933), with turning basin and the developed complex of oil tanks and the Shell refinery beyond, described as 'Manchester's Abadan' by Sylvain Mangeot, 'Manchester's Lifeline', *Picture Post*, 19 February 1955, 22.

poning for ever the contruction of Dock No. 10, which was last mentioned in public in 1926.[17]

The new oil dock was opened to vessels of greater draught by deepening the Ship Canal from Eastham to Stanlow from 28 ft to 30 ft, an improvement authorised in 1924 and completed in 1927. Thereafter the Canal was divided for the first time in its history into two sections of differing depths, respectively five miles and thirty miles in length, and traffic began to focus from 1929 upon the twelve-mile Eastham–Runcorn tidal section where lower tolls were chargeable. Stanlow attracted the leading oil companies, especially Shell and Anglo-American, and acquired tank farms on the south bank of the Canal linked by subterranean pipeline to the oil dock, isolated on the estuary side of the Canal. By 1928 Stanlow ranked second only to London as a port for the import and distribution of petrol and had expanded its storage capacity above that available at the Barton–Mode Wheel end. Shell surpassed Anglo-American in storage capacity by 1929[18] and created a huge centre for distribution by road, rail and Ship Canal. The inflow of petroleum products developed on a large scale. Imports of petrol were first recorded in 1922 and increased at an average annual rate of 18 per cent from 1922 to a peak in 1941, while oil imports increased at a rate of 10 per cent per annum. Those large imports of petrol supplied some compensation for the disappointing progress made in the import of raw cotton and in the export of textiles.[19] Petrol and oil together surpassed timber in tonnage in 1924 and grain in 1925 to become the largest import into the Port of Manchester. In value oil imports rose in importance from the third import to the second in 1930–35 and in 1946–54.

Stanlow became a centre of oil refining from 1924, when Shell-Mex opened its first refinery using crudes imported from Mexico, which ranked as the second largest exporter in the world from 1917

[17] Manchester Ship Canal Company, *Report of the Directors*, 22 February 1926, 4, W. C. Bacon.

[18] Manchester Corporation, *The Official Handbook of Manchester, Salford and District, 1930* (Manchester, 1930), 282.

[19] Manchester Ship Canal Company, *Report of the Directors*, 28 February 1923, 6; 28 February 1924, 7, W. C. Bacon.

to 1928. The development of refining stimulated imports of lead and supplied a new export to the Canal in petrol, which was first recorded in 1923 and expanded in amount almost thrice as fast as petrol imports between 1923 and 1941, surpassing the tonnage of oil exports in 1929–34, 1940 and 1942–45. The Shell refinery was supplemented by others opened by Lobitos Oilfields Ltd in 1934 and by Anglo-American in 1938. The Canal Company proved less successful in developing the traffic of Ellesmere Port, where it built a wharf and transit shed in 1927–28. The shipping conferences, however, defended the interests of Liverpool and prevented the use of the new wharf as a final port of call. In sharp contrast the Stanlow Oil Dock proved so remunerative that a second oil dock was built in 1931–33, in order to eliminate delay in the berthing and discharge of tankers and to handle treble the volume of petrol.[20] The Port of Manchester maintained its position as the second oil port of the kingdom, shipping limited quantities of petrol in special barges along the Ship Canal from 1932 as far as Mode Wheel.

During the war of 1939–45 Stanlow was integrated into a new national system of transportation, being linked by pipeline to Bromborough in 1941, to Avonmouth in 1942 and by a great quadrilateral line to Misterton, Sandy and Aldermaston in 1943, so becoming with Avonmouth one of the twin sources of supply of aviation fuel to the airfields of eastern England. Finally it was linked to the beaches of Normandy in 1944 by the cross-Channel pipeline 'Pluto', which was manufactured in Trafford Park and proved both a technical triumph and a tactical failure. In the post-war period the source of supply of oil shifted sharply from America to the Middle East and the Ship Canal assumed a new importance in the oil trade, importing in 1946 its peak proportion of 24.5 per cent of the nation's imports of crude and an average of 15.74 per cent of those imports between 1946 and 1960.

The Canal Company successfully opposed the attempt by Unilever in 1946 to secure parliamentary sanction for the conversion of

[20] *Manchester Guardian*, 27 May 1933, 11, 14ii, on the opening of Stanlow Oil Dock No. 2 by the Minister of Transport, Oliver Stanley (1896–1950), and on the inaugural entry of the *British Duchess*.

Bromborough Dock, authorised in 1923 and opened in 1931, from a private dock into a general dock designed especially for the oil trade. The Ship Canal entered in 1946 upon an unprecedented period of ten consecutive years of increasing traffic as oil supplied 31 per cent of the increment in import tonnage in 1948. The Middle East replaced the Caribbean as the leading exporter of oil in 1950, linking the traffic of the Ship Canal and the Suez Canal together as the largest flow of crude in history gathered momentum. The use of oil was vastly extended by its adoption in power stations and by the petrochemical revolution. Shell added a chemical plant at Stanlow in 1946–49, so introducing a new industry to the U.K., and then built an immense new oil refinery (1949–51) at a cost of £15 million. Under such stimuli oil established a dominant position in the trade of the waterway never attained by any other commodity. Petroleum products did far more than fill the gap created by the decline of the cotton industry. They boosted total export tonnage from 1950 above the record level of 1907 and rose in status from the third largest export in the years 1930–48 to the second in 1949 and to the first in 1951. Oil imports proved even more important in reviving the transoceanic trade of the Port of Manchester after the wartime depression and in raising its shipping tonnage to unprecedented levels. Imports of crude surpassed those of refined products in tonnage in 1950 and in value in 1951. From 1950 oil and petrol together supplied more than half the aggregate tonnage of imports and from 1952 replaced raw cotton as the most valuable import into the port, so securing in its trade the primacy established in 1944 in the import trade of the kingdom. Shell became the premier client of the Canal Company and the expansion of traffic at the Stanlow terminal reduced the relative importance of the Manchester docks and of its ancillary companies, including Manchester Liners and Trafford Park Estates.

In order to escape from the limitations of the 30 ft depth of the Eastham–Stanlow section the Canal Company decided to build a new oil dock adjacent to the Eastham locks but with its own separate entrance lock from the Mersey estuary. In order to finance the construction of the dock the Company issued in 1951 a £5 million fifteen-year loan under the guarantee of Manchester Corporation, increasing its annual interest payments by 66 per cent from 1952. The dock took four and a half years to build instead of the expected three and cost £5½ million instead of the estimated £4 million. The Queen Elizabeth II Dock was the largest oil dock in Britain, with a depth of 40 ft and an entrance lock 100 ft in width, or 20 ft wider than the Eastham large lock. It was designed for the largest tankers in service, or 'super-tankers' of 30,000 tons in accordance with the estimates of Shell, and was first entered on 19 January 1954 by the Shell tanker *Velletia* of 28,000 tons, laden with crude from Kuwait, Britain's substitute source of supply for Iran after the Abadan crisis.[21] The standard tanker had been one of 10,000–12,000 tons in the 1930s and 1940s but had become one of 16,000–19,000 tons by 1953. The dimensions of the new dock were, however, determined by the size of the 'super-tankers' of 25,000 tons, which had been first built from 1951 under the stimulus of the Abadan crisis.

The Queen Elizabeth II Dock was linked by pipeline to Stanlow, five miles to the east, and handled more imported oil during its first year of operation than the rest of the port, helping to increase imports of petrol by 60 per cent in 1954, imports of oil by 75 per cent and the total traffic of the Canal by 31 per cent. The Port of Manchester regained the position of the second oil port of the kingdom which it had lost to Swansea in the years 1951–53. It found itself committed to the unexpectedly expensive task of dredging a deep approach channel from the Mersey, which had begun from 1951 to suffer from increased siltation. The balance of oil imports tilted decisively in favour of crude from 1954, when the port imported the peak proportion of 15 per cent of the total imports of refined petroleum products into the U.K.

Early in 1956 the Canal Company planned to add a third oil dock to the Stanlow system so as to end the delays experienced by tankers

[21] *Manchester Guardian*, 20 January 1954, 3iii–iv. *Petroleum Times*, 5 February 1954, 113–14. D. C. Milne, 'The Queen Elizabeth II Dock, Eastham', *Proceedings of the Institution of Civil Engineers*, vol. 4 Part 2, 1955, 1–54, 26 October 1954. Port of Manchester, *Queen Elizabeth II Dock* (Manchester Ship Canal Company, 1954, 15 pp.).

and to raise the water level in the tidal section of the Canal from 30 ft to 32 ft, securing the necessary statutory powers. That plan was designed to benefit Shell, which had built Stanlow into the largest of its four British refineries. Shell decided, however, to use even larger super-tankers and to abandon the Queen Elizabeth Oil Dock in favour of the Tranmere Oil Terminal eight miles up the estuary at Birkenhead, which the Mersey Docks & Harbour Board had secured powers in 1956 to construct. The Suez crisis of 1956 produced immediate adverse effects upon the traffic of the Canal and the oil industry of the port. It extended the use of extremely large tankers which could not negotiate even the approach channel to the Queen Elizabeth Dock, let alone the Ship Canal. The Canal Company abandoned its scheme for a third Stanlow oil dock and launched special traffic drives to draw trade from the Midlands and to increase the use of Ellesmere Port. Then the Tranmere jetties were opened, berthing their first tanker with 35,300 tons of crude from Kuwait on 8 June 1960.[22] Those jetties were designed to handle two tankers of 65,000 tons, which were the largest size capable of negotiating the Mersey bar when fully laden. Their competition reduced the oil imports of the Canal by 43 per cent in 1960–61, those of the Queen Elizabeth Dock by 76 per cent and the total tonnage handled by the port by 19.7 per cent from the level reached in the climactic year of 1959.[23] The depression of 1960–61 was concentrated in the oil traffic of the port and bore hardest upon its import trade, bringing to an end the dominance of crude in the total value of oil imports which had been maintained from 1951 to 1962. Refined products surpassed crude imports in both tonnage and value from 1963 and reached a peak in 1964. In the new division of labour created by the Tranmere terminal the port of Liverpool imported crude oil while the port of Manchester increased its exports of refined products from 1963 in both the foreign and coastwise trades, so gaining in the value of its traffic what it lost in quantity. Even at the peak of their relative

22 *Manchester Guardian*, 9 June 1960, 8iii, 16i–ii.

23 The official *Annual Statements of Trade*, in contrast to the more reliable Traffic Statistics of the Canal Company, show that imports of crude reached their peak tonnage in 1956 and their peak value in 1957.

importance in 1959 oil imports had supplied 72 per cent of the tonnage of imports but only 28 per cent of their value.

Shell continued to expand its operations at Stanlow and made increasing use of pipelines for transportation. In 1957 it took over from Petrochemicals Ltd the chemical refinery at Partington and supplied it with feedstock by five pipelines laid in 1957–59 from Stanlow to Partington and Carrington. In 1968 Shell acquired Lankro Chemicals Ltd, which had been established at Eccles in 1937. From 1970 it invested £120 million in a new chemical plant at Carrington, transforming it into one of the largest plants in Europe. Thus it created a vast chemical manufacturing complex to the windward of Manchester and achieved a major expansion in the sphere of its activity. Other product pipelines linked Stanlow to Ince and to Runcorn for bunkering as well as to Haydock for power generation. For the transport of crude Shell linked Stanlow to Heysham by six pipelines, which were laid from 1966 over sixty-eight miles and provoked its rivals, led by Esso, to undertake the construction of a Milford Haven–Manchester pipeline. The Mersey–Thames pipeline was, however, completed in 1969 by U.K. Oil Pipelines Ltd, which was formed by the major oil companies, including Shell. The increase in size of the super-tanker to 200,000 d.w.t. of 62 ft draught in 1966 was accelerated by the Arab-Israeli war of 1967, which closed the Suez Canal for eight years. Such tankers required anchorage terminals of great depth. In 1973–77 Shell therefore completed at a cost of £63 million a seventy-six-mile pipeline to Amlwch in Anglesey,[24] where the largest tankers could berth free from the constraints of the Mersey bar.[25] The reception of the first crude oil from Anglesey at Stanlow in 1977 made possible an expansion in the refinery's capacity by half which made it the largest in Britain, exceeding in throughput even the Esso refinery at Fawley. From the central position of Stanlow Shell could profit by the most highly developed structure of communications in the land, including the new motorways, in order to distribute its products at the lowest possible cost.

[24] *The Times*, 25 February 1977, 4vii–viii; 6 October 1977, 22ii.
[25] *Petroleum Times*, 4 March 1977, 29–32, 'The North Wales Pipeline'.

The industrial development of the banks of the Ship Canal had been expected by the promoters to prove the ultimate financial salvation of the Canal Company and had generated visions of the emergence of a 'city region' or urban province of 'Lancaston' extending from the Mersey to the Pennines. 'In time there would be three or four Manchesters between here [Manchester] and Liverpool.'[26] Those expectations were not fulfilled immediately, as the canalside townships of Eastham, Ellesmere Port, Frodsham, Runcorn, Rixton and Irlam declined in population during the 1890s as they lost the migrant navigators engaged in the construction of the waterway. New centres of industry proved slow to develop and the three established canal ports of Ellesmere Port, Weston and Runcorn continued to serve the trade of the Midlands rather than of Lancashire. The construction of docks at Runcorn and Warrington was postponed in 1895[27] and the reduction of dues on traffic in the tidal section of the Canal proved an insufficient enticement to manufacturers. Above all, Manchester exerted a magnetic attraction through its vast market and labour supply and extended its centripetal influence in the 1900s through the new electric tramways. Even in the Manchester district Barton developed only slowly because of its distance from the main centre of population. By the 1930s, however, a 'Ship Canal Zone' had emerged as a new industrial complex distinct from the older world of 'Cottonia', benefiting the south of Lancashire at the expense of the north and bringing industry into the rural borderland of Lancashire and Cheshire.[28] The explosive development of canalside industry began only with the oil boom of the 1950s and the motorway revolution of the 1960s.

The 'wide bay' of Runcorn had been designated in 1883 as the

[26] *Manchester City News*, 28 November 1896, 8vi, John Glover (1829–1920), ship broker. H. J. Mackinder, *Britain and the British Seas* (Oxford, Clarendon Press, 1902), 275–6. P. Geddes, *Cities in Evolution* (London, Williams, 1915), 31–2. T. W. Freeman, H. B. Rodgers and R. H. Kinvig, *Lancashire, Cheshire, and the Isle of Man* (London, Nelson, 1966), 182–205, 'The Mersey–Irwell Belt'.

[27] B.O.D., 275, 8 March 1895; 323, 10 May; 388, 16 August; 422–3, 11 October 1895.

[28] Manchester Ship Canal Company, *Report of the Directors*, 25 February 1935, 4, F. J. West.

terminal port of a tidal canal but was by-passed under the plan of 1885 in favour of Eastham. It ceased to be an independent port in 1894 and was absorbed within the Port of Manchester. Runcorn remained, however, a great canal port and the main entrepôt of the Bridgewater Canal, handling traffic for Liverpool as well as for the Midlands. It benefited by the existence of the railway bridges higher up the Ship Canal and became a port of discharge until 1905 for timber and grain from sailing vessels for onward lightering to Manchester. The chemical industry developed upon the western and eastern flanks of

The head offices of the Manchester Ship Canal Company.
41 Spring Gardens, Manchester, built in 1890 and occupied from 1891 until 1927.
Ship Canal House, King Street, built in 1924–26 to the design of Harry Smith Fairhurst (1868–1945). This building was the city's first skyscraper, rising to a height of 140 ft and being crowned by a symbolic status of 'Enterprise', but earned no mention in N. Pevsner, *The Buildings of England, Lancashire I* (1969).

the town under the influence of I.C.I., engulfed the tanning trade and made Runcorn into a true sister town of Widnes, to which it was linked by the transporter bridge erected in 1901–05 in place of the former ferry. Runcorn increased in population very slowly until the 1960s, when its docks experienced a revival of activity after they were divorced from the Bridgewater Canal and linked to the Ship Canal. It acquired a Japanese factory in 1970 and a Shopping City as the heart of its 'New Town' in 1972: in 1974 it became the seat of the new borough of Halton, with a larger population than that of Crewe.

To the west of the great Runcorn bend on the Canal a second industrial enclave emerged in rural Cheshire with the development of Ellesmere Port and Stanlow. Ellesmere Port had been established as a canal port in 1795 and became a seaport in 1894, like Runcorn, but was adversely affected by the competition of Garston, developed by the L.N.W.R., which had owned since 1851 the Shropshire Union Railway and Canal Company. The port secured a floating pontoon dock in 1893, provided by Renwick's dry dock company, and began to develop its industrial capacity during the Edwardian era, acquiring three flour mills in 1905–10 and two rolling mills in 1903–05. The Wolverhampton Corrugated Iron Co. Ltd arrived in 1905 and became from 1908 the largest employer of labour in succession to the Shropshire Union Canal, almost doubling the population of the new urban district in 1901–11.[29] Attempts failed, however, to attract shipbuilding, tube manufacture or ore treatment.[30] The Canal Company derived almost no benefit from the toll-free traffic of the port[31] and vainly sought to develop it as a final port of call by dredging the Ship Canal to a depth of 28 ft in 1905 and of 30 ft in 1927. It took over the docks of the Shropshire Union Canal in 1922 and operated them until 1958, when it completed the conversion of the town into a seaport.

Ellesmere Port surpassed Runcorn in population during the 1920s

[29] A. Jarvis, *Ellesmere Port—Canal Town, 1795–1821* (Ellesmere Port, North Western Museum of Inland Navigation Ltd, 1977), 30–3.

[30] B.O.D., 360, 19 October 1906; 60, 13 December 1907; 10–11, 6 January 1911; 44, 3 March 1911.

[31] Ibid., 149, 4 September 1908.

under the dynamic influence of the development of Stanlow and replaced Birkenhead as the growth-point of industry in the Wirral, benefiting by the construction in 1934 of a road link to North Wales and South Lancashire. To its manufacturing establishments it added Bowater's paper mill in 1929 and Vauxhall's car factory in 1958. Vauxhall established an assembly plant in 1961 and became the largest employer in the town in succession to the Wolverhampton Corrugated Iron Company.[32] During the forty years 1931–71 the population of the port trebled while that of Runcorn only doubled. It recruited immigrants from the Irish colony of Liverpool and passed under the influence of the capital of Merseyside. To the east Stanlow Works had been established for the smelting of lead by the Smelting Corporation Ltd (1898–1906)[33] and was then used for the manufacture of cement by the Ship Canal Portland Cement Manufacturers Ltd (1911–32)[34] but found its true destiny in the refining of oil, creating a new town to the south in Thornton le Moors. Ellesmere Port became a boom city in the 1950s and acquired its own new town in Whitby. The traffic of its port first secured the prestige of separate record in the official statistics of trade from 1968. After it acquired a container terminal in 1972 it increased the value of its exports until they exceeded those of Manchester itself from 1976, so ushering in the western phase in the history of the Ship Canal.

[32] *Manchester Guardian*, 20 November 1975, 21v.

[33] B.O.D., 358–9, 11 February 1898; 410, 1 July 1898; 381, 19 April 1901; 79–80, 20 June 1902; 388–9, 28 December 1906.

[34] Ibid., 64–5, 28 April 1911.

8

Conclusion

The canal has been made by faith, which has literally removed mountains. The motive power throughout has been the faith of the masses of the Lancashire population. They believed, not so much in a direct commercial return to the shareholders, as in the value of the canal to the trade of the district. [*The Times*, 1 January 1894, 9iv]

It is to Lancashire what the Nile is to Egypt. [Alfred Watkin, fifth chairman of the Ship Canal Company, on the inauguration of Stanlow Oil Dock No. 2, 26 May 1933]

In 1935 a memorial plaque was unveiled in the foyer of Ship Canal House to Daniel Adamson, who founded his boiler-making works at Dukinfield in 1851 and left behind a unique monument in the Manchester Ship Canal as well as the successor engineering firms of Adamson & Hatchett Ltd of Dukinfield and Joseph Adamson & Co. Ltd of Hyde. The completed waterway differed, however, notably from Adamson's original idea of 'a Lancashire Clyde' in so far as it was a locked canal rather than a tidal cut, it was not financed solely from the savings of small investors and it did not form part of a great highway between the Irish Sea and the North Sea. But it was a typical creation of Mancunian enterprise in so far as it was a wholly new port without any history of gradual development. It was designed for use by general cargo vessels and not by ships carrying luxuries, mail, passengers or pleasure-seekers. The creation of that waterway was accomplished in the face of the most formidable of opposition and gave rise to 'the most protracted struggle ever known in the history of Private Bill legislation'.[1] That resistance lasted for ten full years from 1883 and was overcome by the idealism of local supporters as well as by the investment of capital equivalent to one-tenth of the annual turnover of Manchester's banks in 1893.

From 1894 the forces of opposition mustered anew to deny to the new port the trade it had been built to handle. The Port of Manchester then embarked upon a never-ending career of marketing, selling its facilities in a buyer's market in the most competitive of all worlds. It was the task and the achievement of the Canal Company to acquire and maintain a hinterland in a shipping world dominated by London, Liverpool and Hull. The most important event in the history of the Canal in 1894 was thus neither its formal opening to traffic nor its official inauguration by Queen Victoria but the election of the merchant John K. Bythell as chairman. His dynamic energy raised the status of the port from the sixteenth of 116 customs ports of the U.K. in 1894 to the fourth in 1906, so securing to it the position which it lost only briefly during the decade of depression, 1931–39. Bythell's career proved conclusively that unresting enterprise was essential to enable the port to secure and preserve the traffic appropriate to its geographical position.

The Canal did not succeed in the impossible task of dethroning Liverpool but had never been intended simply to capture the existing trade of a rival. It sought rather to reduce the cost of cargo handling, to transform the framework within which all commercial calculations were made and so to benefit the whole economic world. The creation of the Port of Manchester ushered in a new era in the history of a great city, endowing it with a new and highly specialised sector of economic life oriented towards world commerce and maintaining the cosmopolitan tradition established by the Manchester merchants of the nineteenth century. In a variety of ways it stimulated economic growth, by employing the factors of production in a great construction enterprise, by permanently reducing transport costs, by opening up new careers to talent, by stimulating the engineering trades and by permitting the planting in Trafford Park of a seed-bed

1 *Illustrated London News*, 26 May 1894, 649, 'The Romance of the Ship Canal'.

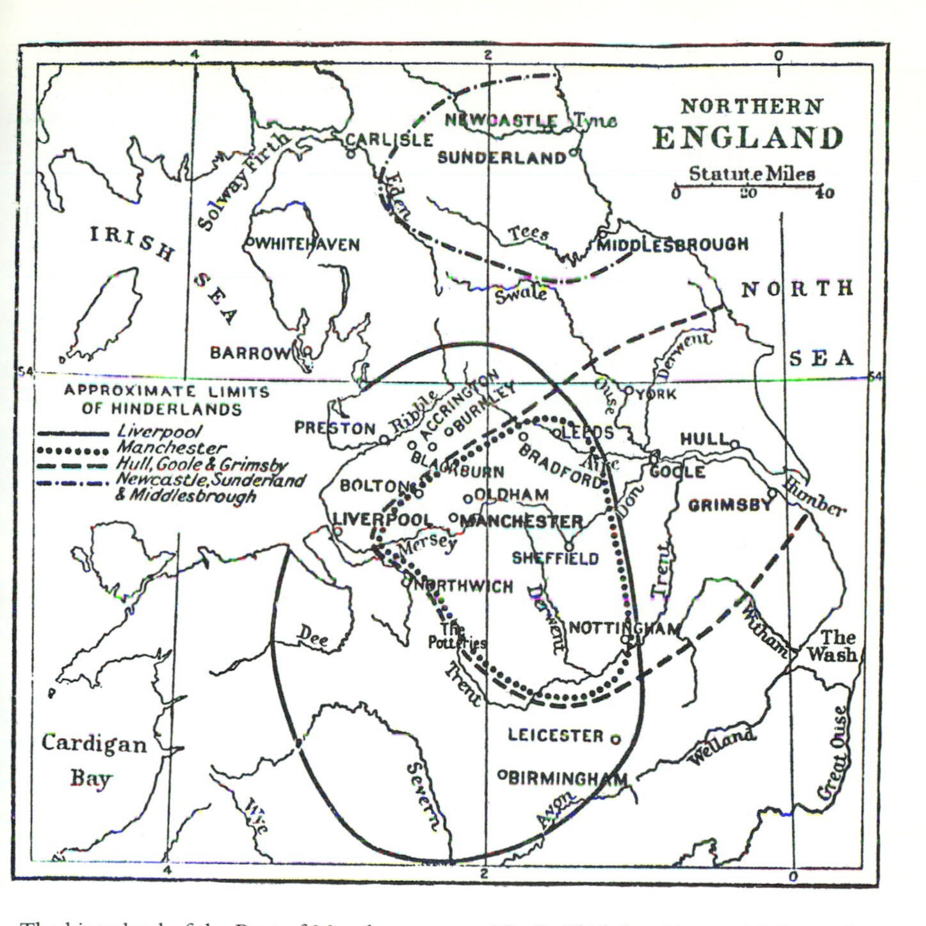

The hinterland of the Port of Manchester, 1904 (*G. C. Chisholm, Commercial Geography, 5th edn., London, Longmans, 1904, 54*). The illustration clearly shows the common hinterland shared by the ports of Liverpool, Hull and Manchester and the absence of any competition between Manchester and the ports of the north-east coast. J. H. Schultze, *Die Häfen Englands* (Leipzig, Deutsche Wissenschaftliche Buchhandlung, 1930), 75, 182, map 2, shows the hinterland of Liverpool in 1925 to have become much more extensive.

of high-technology industry manufacturing intermediate rather than consumer goods. In both construction and operation the port was a creation of capital rather than of labour and it developed a tradition of capital-intensive cargo handling. The increased employment of the population of Lancashire in distribution[2] may have retarded long-term economic development but stemmed from the horizontal reorganisation of the cotton industry and cannot fairly be attributed to the influence of the new port.

The Canal Company successfully adapted its operations to changes in both the economic structure of the country and Britain's position within the world economy. The long-term shift in the economic centre of gravity of the U.K. had begun in the closing decades of the nineteenth century, when Birmingham exceeded Manchester in population during the 1880s and Liverpool during the 1890s.[3] That trend enhanced the influence of London in Lancashire, which had increased through the purchase in 1888–98 of the last independent local banks, through the diligent advertising in 1888–95 of the advantages of the Lancashire industrial area,[5] and through the printing from 1900–09 of northern editions of daily papers. In the post-war decade of the 1920s the 'rationalisation movement' centralised the control of northern industry in the capital. The associated southward shift of the balance of industrial power was accelerated by the decline of the Lancashire cotton industry and by the liberating influence of electric power, of the diesel engine and of road transport. London re-established its supremacy over Liverpool as the leading

[2] T. A. Welton, 'Notes on the Census Report (1901) for the County of Lancaster', *Transactions of the Manchester Statistical Society*, 19 November 1902, 22–3, 32, 42.

[3] B. R. Mitchell and P. Deane, *Abstract of British Historical Statistics* (Cambridge University Press, 1962), 25.

[5] *Manchester of Today, An Epitome of Results. Business Men and Commercial Interests* (London, Historical Publishing Company, 1888, 224 pp.). *Lancashire, the Premier County of the Kingdom. Cities and Towns. Historical, Statistical, Biographical, Business Men and Mercantile Interests* (London, Historical Publishing Company, 1888, 1889, 2 vols., 320 pp., 224 pp.). *The Century's Progress: Lancashire* (London Printing and Engraving Company, 1892, 294 pp.). *Lancashire. Men of the Period. The Records of a Great County – Portraits and Pen Pictures of Leading Men. Part First* (London, Biographical Publishing Company, 1895, 164 pp.).

port of export from 1922 and reasserted its role as the primate port of the land. In contrast the combined share of Liverpool and Manchester in the export trade of the U.K. sank from a peak of 44.4 per cent in 1917 to 11.6 per cent in 1976, while their joint share in the import trade declined from 42.8 per cent in 1918 to 9.4 per cent in 1976.

That shift in economic power was associated with a vast increase in the power of the central government within the country. The State had never been over-friendly towards Mancunian commerce and it regarded the Ship Canal as a private concern rather than as a quasi-public corporation. Thus Lord Rosebery as Foreign Secretary ungraciously declined on 2 September 1893 to notify British consuls abroad of the prospective opening of the new waterway on the grounds that the Foreign Office had no wish to set a precedent.[6] When the Canal was opened it did not fulfil any strategic function, unlike the Kiel Canal. Nor was it ever used by troops except by U.S. soldiers in 1918.[7] Its opening did, however, coincide with the birth of navalist sentiment in Manchester and its facilities made possible regular annual visits to the docks by naval squadrons from 1912.[8]

The potential capacity of the Ship Canal as a national asset was never fully recognised by the State except during the wars of 1914–18 and 1939–45, when the insecurity of the east-coast ports raised Manchester to the rank of the third port of the realm in 1917–18 and again in 1947–48. The wartime services rendered by the Canal Company to the nation were requited by the quadrupling between 1939 and 1945 of its tax payments. The department of State most closely associated with the port reconciled itself only slowly to the existence of a system of inland docks: on two separate occasions, in 1925 and 1959, ill-considered attempts were made to remove the Customs House from the docks to Deansgate in the heart of the city, without due regard to the interests of merchants, ship owners or the Canal Company. Successive bold attempts were even made, in 1931,

[6] B.O.D., 371–3, 15 September 1893.

[7] *Manchester Guardian*, 17 July 1918, 3, 4vi, 'The Americans. On the March through Manchester. Civic Welcome'.

[8] B.O.D., 387, 3 May 1901; 426, 15 March 1907; 274, 26 April; 278, 10 May; 287–8, 7 June 1912.

1947 and 1962, to 'nationalise' the ports, to bring Manchester under the administration of Liverpool and to undo the labours of the founding fathers of the Ship Canal. The Canal Company fought off those challenges and adapted to the concentration of economic activity in south-east England, which continued under the influence of Britain's entry into the E.E.C. in 1973 and the beginning of production of North Sea oil in 1975.

The collective memory of the official nation revealed a myopic failure to assess the achievements of the Ship Canal at their true worth. Even its basic functions earned little recognition in national works of reference. Only two of five multi-volume encyclopaedias in the English language included any article on the Canal. The *New Cambridge Modern History* mentioned it in its eleventh volume (1962) but the *Cambridge Economic History of Europe* (1965, 1978) ignored it. A definitive seven-volume *History of Technology* (1954–78) omitted any reference to what has been described as 'in sheer magnitude . . . the greatest civil engineering achievement of the Victorian age'.[9] The volumes of the *Dictionary of National Biography* published for the period down to 1960 included none of the four chairmen of the Canal Company who succeeded Adamson and Egerton. Such reticence may reflect either a belief that the Canal was simply an enlarged river navigation or a preference for the naval aspect of maritime history, such as was enshrined in a 972-page *Companion to Ships and the Sea* (1976) and in the fifty-eight maritime museums of the kingdom. Thus the National Maritime Museum was founded at Greenwich in 1934 by the scion of a Manchester dynasty, Geoffrey Callender (1875–1946) but included no exhibit relating to the Manchester Ship Canal until 1972. Then the New Neptune Hall was opened and displayed as its central feature the steam paddle tug *Old Trafford* which had served on the Ship Canal from 1907 until 1950.[10]

[9] L. T. C. Rolt, *Victorian Engineering* (London, Allen Lane, 1970), 269.

[10] H. Campbell McMurray, *Old Order New Thing, being a short study of tugs, their men and their machinery, set within the context of the Manchester Ship Canal and with particular reference to the paddle tug*, RELIANT, *formerly* OLD TRAFFORD (London, National Maritime Museum, 1972, 78 pp.). Regrettably the tug was displayed under its final name of *Reliant*.

Such minimal homage to Mancunian enterprise lagged well behind the integration of the Port of Manchester from the 1960s into a new international system of transport.

Perhaps more important for the future was the relative economic decline of Britain as a whole as political and social 'values' were exalted above the economic calculus and ability migrated from the wealth-producing sectors of the economy into a widening range of unproductive bureaucracies parasitic upon the productive sectors. The change in the 'values' of society was reflected in the curious history of the Port Sanitary Authority, which would have been inconceivable in the depressed climate of the 1880s and which inherited the gadfly function of the Joint Rivers Committee. The ambitious paternalism of the new agency threatened repeatedly to do serious injury to the trade of the port in foodstuffs.[11] The decline of the foreign cattle trade of the port from the peak level of 1905–08 cannot have been unrelated to the powers granted to the Port Sanitary Authority in 1906 to inspect foreign meat.

To such challenges the Canal Company responded with unrivalled fertility of resource and with the solid support of the Corporation of Manchester. It also adapted its strategy to the transport revolution effected by the triumph of road over rail haulage, by the advent of the motorway and the intermodal container, and by the severing in 1972 of the old rail connection to the docks. From 1957 the Company began to adapt its services to road transport by establishing a Quay Delivery Bureau for import traffic. From 1962 it waged an export drive and extended its interests in the transport and handling of goods, encouraging from 1965 the palletisation of export traffic. In 1968 it established a Container Terminal complete with consolidation depot at North No. 9 Dock on the site once destined for Dock No. 10. That innovation elaborated the Mancunian tradition of the capital-intensive handling of cargo and set in motion the greatest change in cargo handling ever made, slashing costs to a new

[11] Port of Manchester, *Annual Report of Medical Officer of Health to the Port Sanitary Authority, 1906* (Manchester, Snape, 1907), 59–76. B.O.D., 281, 30 March 1906; 283, 6 April; 304, 18 May; 307–8, 1 June; 325, 13 July; 390, 28 December 1906; 237, 2 April 1909; 320, 12 November 1909.

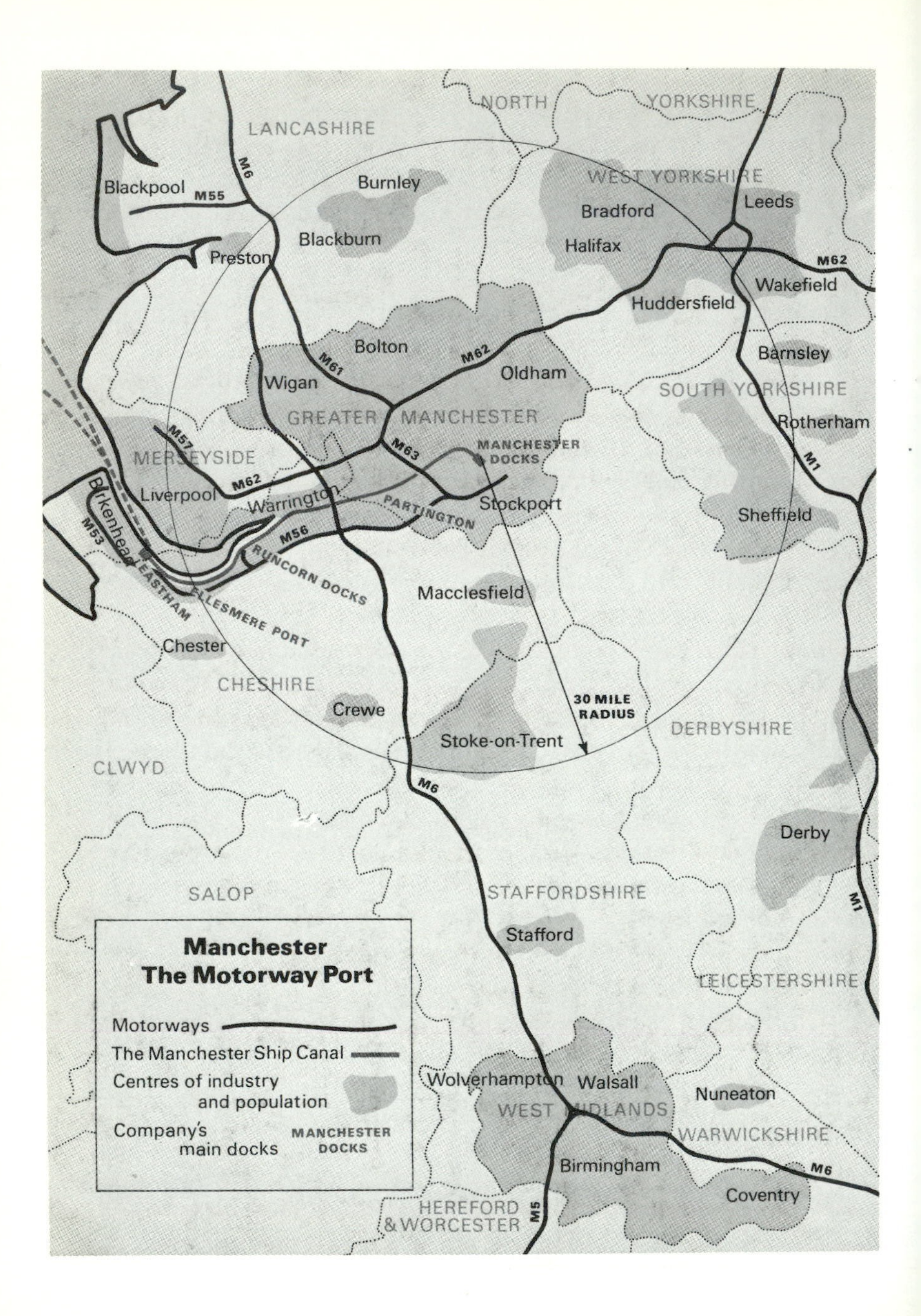
Manchester
The Motorway Port
Motorways
The Manchester Ship Canal
Centres of industry and population
Company's main docks
MANCHESTER DOCKS
NORTH YORKSHIRE
LANCASHIRE
WEST YORKSHIRE
GREATER MANCHESTER
MERSEYSIDE
SOUTH YORKSHIRE
CHESHIRE
DERBYSHIRE
CLWYD
SALOP
STAFFORDSHIRE
LEICESTERSHIRE
WEST MIDLANDS
WARWICKSHIRE
HEREFORD & WORCESTER
Blackpool
Preston
Burnley
Blackburn
Bradford
Halifax
Leeds
Wakefield
Huddersfield
Barnsley
Rotherham
Sheffield
Bolton
Wigan
Oldham
Liverpool
Birkenhead
Warrington
Stockport
PARTINGTON
RUNCORN DOCKS
EASTHAM
ELLESMERE PORT
Macclesfield
Chester
Crewe
Stoke-on-Trent
30 MILE RADIUS
Derby
Stafford
Wolverhampton
Walsall
Nuneaton
Birmingham
Coventry
M6
M55
M61
M62
M63
M57
M53
M56
M1
M5

The motorway port of Manchester, 1975 (*Manchester Ship Canal Company*). The map shows the carefully planned system of motorways flanking the Ship Canal and linking Lancashire to Yorkshire, the Midlands and the north. Two high-level bridges were built across the Ship Canal, at Barton (1957–60) and Thelwall (1959–63). The Stretford–Eccles by-pass, M62, was 'the first classified road in Britain to have the status of a motorway' (J. O. Drake, *Motorways*, London, Faber, 1969, 145–7, 205–6).

---

minimum. By making full use of the customs privileges of the Port of Manchester and turning the newly completed Lancashire and Yorkshire motorway to its own advantage the Company sharply increased the share of exports in the total trade of the port from 1971. It extended the technique of containerisation westwards to Warrington, to Runcorn and to Ellesmere Port. The pattern of traffic fluctuations altered as the value of cargo handled increased year by year, despite recessions in its volume in 1970, 1972 and 1975. In 1973 the Company established Bridgewater Transport Services Ltd, sold off its last barges in 1974 and so transformed its most historic department into a road haulage concern. Thus it boldly undertook the total transformation of a modern railway port into a modern motorway port.

From 1963 the Canal Company began to pay respectable ordinary dividends which surpassed those of Manchester Liners in 1967–73 and those of Trafford Park Estates in 1969–73. Over the ninety-four years 1885–1978 the Company paid an average ordinary dividend of 3.4 per cent: during the ten years 1969–78 it paid one of 13.3 per cent to some 14,000 shareholders. That achievement was all the greater because of the slower turnover of its capital in contrast to that of manufacturing enterprises,[12] the very high cost of dredging created by the process of long-term geological change, and the impact of the world depression of 1973–79.

The Canal fulfilled certain secondary functions as well as its primary one. As a deep barrier excavated in the channel of the Irwell and Mersey it created a new civic boundary between Salford and

[12] In 1965 the Ship Canal Company was the 145th of 300 industrial companies ranked by capital employed but in 1970 it was the 600th of 1,000 ranked by turnover. *The Times 300* (London, The Times, 1965), 6. *The Times 1,000, 1970–71* (London, The Times, 1970), 38.

Manchester and replaced the Mersey as the 'boundary river' between Lancashire and Cheshire from Flixton to Warrington from 1914 until the reorganisation of local government in 1974.[13] Although it was used by humble sludge steamers as well as by large ocean liners, the Canal continued to exert a powerful appeal to the imagination.[14] As a monument to local patriotism and 'the pride of Northern England',[15] as an immense feat of engineering and the aorta of Lancashire, the Canal attracted to its banks, and especially to Barton Aqueduct, the pilgrims and the image-makers of a technological civilisation.[16] Educational trips along the waterway were first devised by Captain Bacon in 1928 for the benefit of the Company's employees and were extended to the general public in 1934. The educational function of the Canal may have been modified by the opening of the two high-level road bridges in 1960–63. The continuing popularity of excursions along the waterway nevertheless paid homage to the gigantic achievement of an earlier generation. The Canal remained not only a seaway into the industrial heartland of Great Britain but also a working memorial to one of the greatest ages in British history.

[13] B.O.D., 58, 21 November 1890; 69, 5 December 1890; 147–8, 30 January 1914.

[14] Manchester Ship Canal Company, *Report of the Directors*, 23 February 1931, 1, A. Watkin.

[15] *Manchester City News*, 16 March 1895, 5iii, Sir Courtenay Boyle, permanent secretary of the Board of Trade.

[16] A triad of films was made in 1924 on the Ship Canal, Trafford Park and the Ford Motor Company. The earliest radio programme on the Ship Canal was broadcast by the B.B.C. on 13 December 1935 and the first television programme on 29 June 1979.

Table 9

The position of the Port of Manchester in the rank order of the customs ports of the U.K. according to the amount of its trade and shipping, 1894–1964

Year	*Value of imports*	*Value of exports*	*Value of imports and exports*	*Shipping tonnage entering*
1894	17	10	16	28
1895	16	7	11	23
1896	13	7	9	20
1897	13	7	9	21
1898	12	7	8	21
1899	11	8	8	20
1900	5	9	6	19
1901	5	9	6	20
1902	6	8	6	18
1903	4	8	6	16
1904	4	5	5	15
1905	4	5	5	13
1906	4	7	4	12
1907	4	6	4	12
1908	4	5	5	12
1909	4	5	4	14
1910	4	6	4	13
1911	4	5	4	13
1912	4	5	4	11
1913	4	8	4	11
1914	4	5	4	15
1915	4	5	5	13
1916	4	5	5	14
1917	3	4	3	14
1918	3	3	3	14
1919	3	4	4	15
1920	3	4	3	13
1921	4	5	5	13
1922	4	4	4	17

Year	*Value of imports*	*Value of exports*	*Value of imports and exports*	*Shipping tonnage entering*
1923	4	4	4	15
1924	4	4	4	14
1925	4	4	3	12
1926	4	5	4	11
1927	4	6	4	11
1928	4	6	4	11
1929	4	6	4	12
1930	4	6	4	12
1931	4	6	5	12
1932	4	6	5	13
1933	4	6	5	13
1934	4	6	5	13
1935	4	6	5	13
1936	4	6	5	12
1937	4	6	5	13
1938	4	6	5	13
1939	4	6	6	
1946	4	4	4	
1947	4	4	3	
1948	3	4	3	
1949	4	5	4	6
1950	4	5	4	7
1951	4	6	4	7
1952	4	6	4	6
1953	4	6	4	6
1954	4	6	4	4
1955	4	6	4	4
1956	4	6	3	4
1957	4	6	3	4
1958	3	6	3	4
1959	3	5	3	4
1960	3	5	4	5
1961	4	6	4	6
1962	4	5	4	6

Year	*Value of imports*	*Value of exports*	*Value of imports and exports*	*Shipping tonnage entering*
1963	4	5	5	5
1964	4	5	4	6

Note. The figures indicate Manchester's relative position in the list of the 116 customs ports which existed in the United Kingdom. Thus '4' means that Manchester ranked fourth after London, Liverpool and Hull. The limitations of the various criteria for ranking ports have been examined by J. Bird, *The Major Seaports of the United Kingdom* (London, Hutchinson, 1963), 21–6. Comparative figures for cargo tonnage exist only from 1964, while comparative shipping tonnage statistics exist not as a single continuous series but as three separate series for the years 1894–1903, 1907–38 and 1949–64, so that the rank shown above for the years 1904–06 has been derived by interpolation. The use of shipping tonnage may be the best criterion for ranking ports on an international basis but benefits unduly transit ports like Harwich and Dover and is especially unfavourable to a port such as Manchester without any passenger trade and located at the head of a long and locked inland navigation. The use of steam shipping tonnage from foreign ports might serve as a more acceptable criterion but would exclude the sail traffic of Runcorn during the first decades of the port's operation and can be used only for the years 1894–1903 and 1907–14, for which figures are available.

The use of customs revenue as a criterion discriminates in favour of the major ports such as London and Liverpool which handled the bulk of dutiable imports and against general cargo ports such as Manchester. Trade values provide the sole continuous series of statistics but exclude the value of coasting trade, which supplied 37 per cent of Manchester's shipping in 1894–1913: such a series is best considered in conjunction with one of net register tonnage.

Source: Annual Statement of Trade, 1894–1964. *Annual Statement of Navigation and Shipping*, 1894–1938. *Board of Trade Journal*, 1951–69. *Digest of Port Statistics*, 1966, 1969.

Select bibliography

One of the great difficulties which the Canal has to encounter is the fact that almost everything that is done gets into the papers somehow or other. [Manchester Ship Canal Company, *Minutes of the Board of Directors*, Vol. 6, 232, 18 January 1895, John K. Bythell.]

No published work has ever sought to make use of the large mass of sources available in print. The existence of those extensive materials reflects a deep and continuing public interest in a great enterprise, an interest far surpassing that displayed in any other concern. Much of the raw material was bequeathed to the Manchester Central Library by Sir Bosdin Thomas Leech (1836–1912) from his 'unique collection of materials, correspondence, reports and records of every kind' (Leech, vol. i, p. vii). The collection is not catalogued separately but forms the core of the unrivalled stock of Ship Canal materials in the Central Library: it should be distinguished from the Leech collection of medical biographies in the Medical Library of the University of Manchester, built up by the son of Bosdin, Dr Ernest Bosdin Leech (1875–1950), nephew of Daniel John Leech (1840–1900), Professor of Materia Medica (1881–1900). The best bibliography of the subject is contained in James Bird, *The Major Seaports of the United Kingdom* (London, Hutchinson, 1963, 1969), 273–6.

One work has remained the primary source used by all later writers, including J. H. Clapham[1] in his *Economic History of Modern Britain* (Cambridge University Press, 1938), vol. 3, 365–9, and A. Redford in his *History of Local*

[1] The historian's father, John Clapham (1822–97), goldsmith, of the firm of John Hall & Co., (1832–1959), diamond merchants and jewellers, of King Street, is recorded by Leech, i, 205, as an early opponent of the Ship Canal scheme in the interests of his fellow ratepayers.

Government in Manchester (London, Longmans, 1940), vol. 2, 353–76, and in the work which B. W. Clapp helped Redford to write, *Manchester Merchants and Foreign Trade* (Manchester University Press, 1956), vol. 2, *1850–1939*, 158–85. B. T. Leech, *History of the Manchester Ship Canal from its Inception to its Completion with Personal Reminiscences* (Manchester, Sherratt, 1907, 2 vols., 333 pp., 315 pp.) was completed when the author was over seventy years of age. Sir Bosdin Leech was well qualified to relate the history of the Canal from 1882 to 1894: he was a member of the Provisional Committee (1882–84), auditor of the Canal Company (1885–92), and mayor of Manchester in 1891–92 after the crisis of 1890–91 in the company's fortunes. For the last twenty years of his life (1892–1912) he served as a Corporation director of the Canal Company. The undoubted merits of the superbly illustrated work were, however, concealed from the editor of the *Manchester Guardian*, C. P. Scott, who published as a first leader a hypercritical review written in a very peevish tone.[2] Scott's judgement was moderated only slightly after the author's death, when he concluded that the work 'though artless, is an inexhaustible mine of information',[3] so damning it with the very faintest of praise. Leech's history remained scrupulously faithful to Scott's own primary tenet of faith as a journalist in its meticulous separation of fact and comment. Scott complained, however, that Leech treated early critics of the scheme as malevolent influences. Scott himself had been one of those opponents from 1882 until 1886,[4] when he was converted under the influence of the merchant J. A. Beith (Leech, i, 323–4; ii, 97–8). His initial hostility was recorded by Leech for the benefit of posterity. Presumably Scott was mortified by the indiscretion of the author in disclosing his opposition to the liberal spirit of the age and in exposing his error of judgement to critical scrutiny. His own hypersensitivity had always led him to shun the publicity which he accorded so freely to others. His vanity may have prompted his ludicrous claim to have been one of the originators of the Canal and may also have been wounded by a personal reflection of the author ('he [Scott] had a flash of genius – such things come to the biggest of fools sometimes', Leech, i, 324). Hence perhaps his curious view of Leech as 'obstinate and opinionated'[3] and his unworthy review of an important book.

[2] *Manchester Guardian*, 7 September 1907, 8i–iii.

[3] Ibid., 17 April 1912, 8iii.

[4] Ibid., 26 March 1883, 5i–ii, a favourable review of the second edition of A. D. Provand's critical pamphlet, *The Manchester Ship Canal Scheme* (Manchester, Heywood, 1882, 76 pp.).

This bibliography excludes works relating to the period of agitation but should identify the two most famous pamphleteers of 1882 – 'Cottonopolis' or Joseph Lawrence (1848–1919), and 'Mancuniensis' or James W. Harvey (1852–98). On the construction of the waterway the indispensable sources are the essays by the engineer himself, Sir Edward Leader Williams (1828–1910), in the *Proceedings of the Institution of Mechanical Engineers*, July 1891, 418–27, 457–61, in the *Transactions of the Manchester Association of Engineers*, 1895, 1–22, in the *Minutes of the Proceedings of the Institution of Civil Engineers*, vol. 131, Session 1897–98, Part i, 3–88, and in the *Encyclopaedia Britannica* (Cambridge University Press, 1911, eleventh edition), xvii, 550–1, together with the long article in *Engineering*, 26 January 1894, 97–142, reprinted (London, *Engineering*, 1894, 46 pp. with four plates). Of several photographic collections the most substantial is *The Manchester Ship Canal, A Pictorial Record of its Construction, 11th November, 1887 to 1st January, 1894. Original Photographs and Notes by G. Herbert Bayley, A.M.Inst.C.E., and Horace C. Bayley* (Manchester, Cornish, 1894, 2 vols., 62 plates from original negatives by G. H. Bayley and H. C. Bayley).

The Public Relations Department of the Ship Canal Company, which was created in 1926, has produced a distinguished series of surveys of the Port of Manchester, including *Manchester and the Sea* (1927, 28 pp., with a text perhaps contributed by W. Haslam Mills), *Resolution and Achievement* (1954, 24 pp.) and *Past and Present* (1978, 24 pp.) There is no history of the dockers but one collective social survey exists in the University of Liverpool, Department of Social Science, *The Dock Worker. An Analysis of Conditions of Employment in the Port of Manchester* (University Press of Liverpool, 1954, 283 pp.), carried out by Joan Woodward, R. S. Webster, Enid Mumford, J. Gogarty and Elizabeth Gittus. There is another social survey of the Regent and Ordsall Park wards of Salford in Barbara N. Stancliffe (Mrs B. N. Rodgers) and Mary S. Muray, 'Till We Build Again', *Social Welfare*, VII: 4, October 1948, 78–108. I have not used the theses on Ellesmere Port by T. W. Roberts (1964) and P. J. Aspinall (1972) or that on Runcorn by A. S. Hope (1978).

The best introduction to the industrial history of Trafford Park remains T. H. G. Stevens, *Some Notes on the Development of Trafford Park, 1897–1947* (Manchester, 1947, 32 pp.): the value of Appendix A, 'Firms taking land in Trafford Park, 1897–1947', has been enhanced by the absence of any surviving series of the *Directory of Firms* (Trafford Park, Manchester, 1933–70). Relevant business histories include those of Metro-Vickers by J. D. Dummelow (1949), of Hedley's (Procter & Gamble) by Patric Dickinson

(1959) and of the British Electric Car Co. Ltd by J. H. Price (1978). Denis Gill, *Transport Treasures of Trafford Park* (Glossop, Transport Publishing Company, 1973, 98 pp.) provides an impressive photographic souvenir of the transport exhibition held at the docks in 1973 as part of the Festival of Manchester.

Manuscript sources

Beaumont Papers, six parcels listed at DDBe in the Lancashire Record Office, Preston, and deposited by John W. G. Beaumont, who was secretary to Marshall Stevens in 1883–84 and a clerk in the head office of the Canal Company from 1885 to 1919, serving as confidential secretary to J. K. Bythell.

De Trafford Papers, unlisted at DDTr in the Lancashire Record Office. The box labelled 'Ship Canal. Railways. Norfolk & Leicestershire' contains a file of correspondence with J. R. Chadderton on the second Manchester Ship Canal Shareholders' Association, 1915–17.

Manchester Association of Importers and Exporters, *Minutes*, 1908–35, 11 vols., M8/6/1–11*

Manchester Chamber of Commerce, *Minutes of the Port of Manchester Committee*, 1935–41, 1946, 1949, M8/5/24, 28, 32, 36, 40, 42, 44, 54, 60*

Manchester Corporation, *Proceedings of Special Committees*, vols. 2–5, 27 August 1890–17 January 1908, 4 vols.

Manchester Cotton Association, *Minutes of the Board*, 1894–1917, 11 vols., M26/1/1–11; 1926–49, 11 vols., M26/1/18–29*

Manchester Cotton Association, *Minutes of the Central Sales Bureau*, 1908–30, M26/6/1*

Manchester Cotton Association, *Register of Members, 1894–1962*, M26/11/3/1*

Manchester Liners Ltd, *Minute Books*, 5 May 1898–20 September 1939, 3 vols.

Manchester Liners Ltd, *Shareholders' Minute Books*, 26 August 1898–13 June 1978, 2 vols.

Manchester Ship Canal Company, *Minute Books of the Board of Directors*, 11 August 1885–5 November 1915, 13 vols., in typescript from 2 July 1915

* On deposit in the Archives Department of the City of Manchester Central Library.

Manchester Ship Canal Company, *Minutes of the Traffic Land and Parliamentary Committee*, which became on 12 June 1893 the *Traffic and Rates Committee*, 21 December 1891–9 February 1900, 4 vols.
Manchester Steamship Lines Association, *Correspondence and Minutes*, 16 February 1894–29 September 1897, M44*
Manchester Timber Trade Association, *Minute Books*, 22 March 1917–8 November 1971, 8 vols. for the period to 17 September 1962 with unbound minutes for the period 25 February 1963–8 November 1971
Royal Commission on Historical Manuscripts, *Report on the Records of Ships Registered at Manchester 1894–1913*, (1973), M110*
Parkyn Papers, listed at DDX 101 in the Lancashire Record Office and deposited by Daniel Adamson Parkyn in 1948.
Salford Corporation, *Minutes of Special Committees*, 14 February 1884–1 June 1894, 2 vols.

The traffic of the Port of Manchester

The indispensable source for the commercial history of the Canal during the first two years of operation is the monthly Traffic Reports of John K. Bythell, which were the forerunners of the chairman's monthly report to the board of directors. The first is dated 30 May 1894, covers the first four months of operation and appears in B.O.D., 87–97, 8 June 1894, as well as in the *Manchester Guardian*, 9 June 1894, 9ii–v. For sixteen months from September 1894 until December 1895 the reports were entered in full in the minutes of the board of directors for the following month. The Traffic Report for September 1894 appears in B.O.D., 161–78, 19 October 1894, and that for December 1895, which includes a full discussion of the traffic of 1894 and 1895, appears in B.O.D., 31–48, 17 January 1896. The last four reports for September–December 1895 include ancillary reports upon the Bridgewater Canal, which was also the subject of a confidential report to the board by John K. Bythell, 'Report and Appendices on Bridgewater Revenue and Traffic' (35 pp., including fifteen appendices, 11 January 1902).

Annual Statements of Navigation and Shipping, 1894–1938
Annual Statements of the Trade of the United Kingdom, 1894–1975. This fundamental source records the commodity traffic passing through the port in vol. 2 (1903–18), vol. 4 (1920–35), vol. 1 (1939), vol. 4 – Supplement (1948–62) and vol. 5 (1963–74). It shows the trade of Ellesmere

Port, Runcorn and Manchester separately from 1968 and was succeeded in 1976 by the annual *Statistics of Trade through United Kingdom Ports*.

Manchester Association of Importers and Exporters, *Annual Reports*, 1908–28, by J. S. McConechy, in the Manchester Chamber of Commerce.

Manchester Corporation, [Miscellaneous Corporation Reports on the Manchester Ship Canal, 1883–1906, including the annual *Reports of the Ship Canal Committee*, 1892–1906, compiled by G. H. Hill, the Corporation Engineer, until 1898 and by Alderman J. W. Southern from 1899.]

Manchester Cotton Association Ltd, *Cotton*, 20 April 1895–28 August 1965, 195 issues.

— *Reports of Shareholders' Meetings*, 1895–1949, M26/7/1–4

— *Raw Cotton Imports into Manchester* [for the forty-five seasons from 1894–95 to 1938–39, together with 1948–49], compiled in March 1939 by Harry Robinson (1880–1963), Secretary of the Manchester Cotton Association from 1912 to 1952, M26/Add/10/2

— *Minute Book of the Protective Committee*, No. 3, 173–4, 10 November 1914, 'Particulars of Cotton Imports to Manchester' [for the twenty seasons from 1894–95 to 1913–14], M26/3/3

Manchester Ship Canal Company, *Port of Manchester. Facts and Figures*, 1971, biennial.

— *Report of the Directors and Statements of Account*, 1886–1972

— *Report of Shareholders' Meetings*, 1886–1963, half-yearly from 1886, annual from 1913, including some early reports by J. K. Bythell which are more informative than the minutes of the board of directors.

— *Report and Accounts*, including the Chairman's Statement to the Shareholders, 1972–77

— *Traffic Statistics*, 1894–1964, reprinted for 1895–1904 in *Manchester Guardian*, 30 December 1905, 27ii–iii

National Ports Council, *Digest of Port Statistics*, 1966–73, including in the volumes for 1966–69 shipping statistics for the years 1956–65

— *Annual Digest of Port Statistics*, 1973–77

Port of Manchester, Port Sanitary Authority, *Annual Report of the Medical Officer of Health*, 1901–38, 1961–73

Allen, G. C., Hyde, F. E., Morgan, D. J., Corlett, W. J., *The Import Trade of the Port of Liverpool. Future Prospects*, 109 pp., University Press of Liverpool, 1946

Barker, W. H., and Fitzgerald, W., 'The City and Port of Manchester', *Journal of the Manchester Geographical Society*, 8 December 1925, 11–31

Cochrane, D. B., Collection of Nautical Press Cuttings in 204 vols., including 3 vols. on the Port of Manchester, 1920–73, deposited in the Lancashire Record Office in 1979 and listed at DDX/1242/4.

Deiss, E., *À Travers l'Angleterre Industrielle et Commerciale* (*Notes de Voyage*), 190–211, Paris, Guillaumin, 1898, based upon information supplied by B. I. Belisha, who was not only the son of David Belisha, a large investor in the Canal Company, but also the uncle of Leslie Hore-Belisha (1893–1957). For the obituary of B. I. Belisha see *Manchester Guardian*, 29 September 1906, 8vii

Fletcher, A. W., 'The Economic Results of the Ship Canal on Manchester and the Surrounding District', *Transactions of the Manchester Statistical Society*, 10 February 1897, 83–108: July 1899, 155–69, with discussion reported in *Manchester City News*, 13 February 1897, 5vi–vii

Galloway, J. R., 'Shipping Rings and the Manchester Cotton Trade', *Journal of the Manchester Geographical Society*, July 1898, 241–63

Hyde, F. E., *Liverpool and the Mersey. An Economic History of a Port, 1700–1970*, 134–41, Newton Abbot, David & Charles, 1971

Hyde, F. E., and Harris, J. R., *Blue Funnel: a History of Alfred Holt and Company of Liverpool from 1865 to 1914*, 105–10, Liverpool University Press, 1956

Law, Alice, 'Social and Economic History', in W. Farrer and J. Brownbill (eds.), *Victoria History of the County of Lancaster*, ii, 323–5, 329, London, Constable, 1908

Leech, B. T., [Press Cuttings on the Manchester Ship Canal], 19 vols., especially vol. 12 (March–April 1894) and vols. 16–19 (1894–1902)

McConechy, J. S., *Direct Trade between New Zealand and Manchester*, 10 pp., Wellington, New Zealand Times, 1905

— 'The Economic Value of the Ship Canal to Manchester and District', *Transactions of the Manchester Statistical Society*, 13 November 1912, 2–126, with fifty-four tables and eighteen charts on pp. 39–126, with discussion in *Manchester City News*, 16 November 1912, 8vii

— 'The Manchester Ship Canal. From Historic Economic and Trade Aspects', *Manchester Rotary Life*, August 1915, 773–87.

— 'The Port of Manchester. What the Ship Canal has done for Manchester', *The Draper's Organiser* (*Manchester Number*), November 1917, 137–41

M'Farlane, J., 'The Port of Manchester: the Influence of a Great Canal', *Geographical Journal*, November 1908, 496–503

Manchester Ship Canal Conference, *The Voice of the Trader*, 38 pp., Manchester, 1896, reviewed in *Manchester City News*, 26 September 1896, 4vii

Mountfield, S., *Western Gateway. A History of the Mersey Docks and Harbour Board*, 41–96, Liverpool University Press, 1965

Pease, A. J., and McKerrow, W. J., *Manchester and Colonial Steamship Co. A Scheme to bring the North of England into Direct Communication with The Cape of Good Hope and the Australasian Colonies*, 12 pp., Manchester, 1894

Samuelson, J., 'The Manchester Ship Canal. Its Present Position and Probable Future', *Liverpool Daily Post*, 16 July 1894, 7vii; 21 July 1894, 3viii

Stevens, M., 'The Manchester Ship Canal as a Factor in Transport', *Journal of the Institute of Transport*, January 1921, 99–113

Stoker, R. B., *Fifty Years on the Western Ocean*, 20 pp., Manchester Liners Ltd, 1948, reprinted from *Sea Breezes*, 1948, and reprinted in revised form as *Sixty Years on the Western Ocean*, 40 pp., 1958

Tracy, W. B., 'The Manchester Ship Canal in its Relation to the Industrial Progress of Manchester', *Trade and Industry*, 31 March 1900, 417–26

Young, T. M., *Manchester and the Atlantic Traffic*, 88 pp., London, Sherratt, 1902, reprinting seven articles from the *Manchester Guardian*, 24 July–20 August 1902, by its Ship Canal correspondent. For the obituary of T. M. Young (1873–1946) see the *Manchester Guardian*, 15 June 1946, 3iii

Index